# PRAISE FOR

*People Buy From People* captures the soul of effective connection. Brian Sexton builds on his late father's amazing legacy by reminding people everywhere that success in business and life comes from a deep appreciation for the only thing that matters -- relationships."

*--Blake Binns, CEO of Good Advice Coaching*
*and Host of the Good Advice Podcast*

In a digitized, automated, and quantified world, what people crave is personal connection. As the gap between true humanity and automation grows, a unique opportunity exists for those willing to gift intentional time to others. I've often commented in podcasts and articles that "people buy from people, not faceless companies." It's exciting that Brian and his late father, Jerry, are educating the world on the win-win benefits of that exact mentality, through *People Buy From People.*

*--Damon Burton, CEO of SEO*
*National and Author of Outrank*

Brian shares the legacy of lessons he learned from his father and it shows in everything he is. *People Buy From People* dives deep into principles that build strong foundations for intentional relationship building and reminds us what life and busines are all about—People.

*--Lori Knudsen, YouMap Certified Coach*
*and President, Knowbility Consulting*

Stories are how we connect at a human level. With mastery, Brian will have you looking inward with your relationships. Deep meaningful connections are intentional, purposeful and empathetic. In *People Buy From People*, Brian has outlined the keys to successfully building human relationships.

*--Larry Levine, Author of Selling From the Heart*

Brian is a natural connector. From the first time I engaged with Brian, he has always been thoughtful in interactions. *People Buy From People* is a showcase of those skills innate in Brian and how those same skills can be showcased in your life as well.

*--Jason Romano, Author of Live to Forgive*
*and The Uniform of Leadership.*

We've all experienced cold pitches form people who skip relationship building and go straight for a sale. Not Brian. He knows and understands connection comes first. Brian offers a refreshing, more effective alternative to selling and connecting in People Buy From People.

*--Kristin A. Sherry, International Best-Selling*
*Author and Creator of YouMap®*

Brian has been an incredible friend for over a decade. I've watched him directly exhibit every skill he details in this book with many types of people. *People Buy from People* is a way of life for Brian, so it's natural that this book is an intentional guide that help people connect and influence their audience.

*--Brian Willett, Sales Trainer, Business*
*Coach and Author of Seven Ways to More*

# PEOPLE BUY FROM PEOPLE

10 Powerful People Lessons from
the Ultimate People Person

*My Dad*

BRIAN SEXTON

ISBN-13:
ISBN-10:

# TABLE OF CONTENTS

# Special Thanks

There are far too many people to thank who have impacted my life, but there are those who deserve Special thanks.

*Tonya, my beautiful wife and partner. Thank you for putting up with me through this and believing in this, though, you didn't understand what I was writing and allowing me to write, at times, about our life together. I love you with all my heart and thank you for the last 24 amazing years. You are the greatest treasure of my life and here's to decades more life and love with you.

*Bryce, my only son. You are an incredible man in the making and I am proud of you beyond words. I can't believe you are my son. I love you so much and hope I've made the same impact on you like your Pap did on me. You are destined for greatness.

*Debbie Sexton Moss, my incredible Mom. The stories I told of Dad; you were in all of them. To be a faithful wife, mother, grandmother, daughter, sister and friend takes someone amazing. You are all that and so much more. I love you and thank you for being the best Mom I could've had.

*Susie Fry, my incredible Mother-in-Law. Thank you and Larry for giving me Tonya and raising an amazing woman. You have always loved me like your own and hope you're proud of the husband and father I am to your daughter and grandson. I love you!

*Ron Moss, my unbelievable Step-father. You stepped in to our family when we needed you most. You have always been the best example of grace and stability. I love you so much!

*Kelley, Lauren, Tina, Sophie, Billy and Brad. My family. Kell, Thank you for the pictures! Thank you all for your love and support all these years. I hope this gives you a greater glimpse into why I am the way I am! I love you all!

*Braley, Allie, Carli, Xander and Xzavier. Someday, you may want to read your Uncle's book. I hope so. You'll learn more about your incredible Pap. I wish you could have gotten more time with him. He loved you all so much and I know he's looking down on you with pride.

*Dale Dupree, Leader of The Sales Rebellion and an incredible friend. Thank you for stepping up for me and writing the forward. You were the right guy and your friendship is a gift. We've talked a bunch about the influence of our dads in our lives that connects us. I wish you, me, Curtis Dupree and Jerry Sexton could break bread together. In Heaven, we will. Love you, brother and thank you so very much.

*Al and Lisa Robertson, Authors, Speakers and Podcasters., our precious friends. Reading your vulnerability in *A New Season* and *Desperate Forgiveness* helped me understand how to be transparent and tap into my emotions while telling the stories of my Dad. Your example was so valuable and I am eternally so grateful for your friendship.

*Kristin A. Sherry, I am incredibly grateful for your friendship. You were a Beta Reader, Endorser, confidant, encourager and gave me wise counsel. You were always a phone call or text away when I needed help. Thank you from the bottom of my heart.

*Eric Konovalov, you told me I could do this. Without that conversation in the parking lot of Home Depot in Barboursville, WV, this book doesn't happen. You told me this: "B, you're uncomfortable because you're in the Growth zone and there's no growth in your Comfort zone." What profound wisdom. Thank you, EK.

*Kim Thompson-Pinder, Eric Konovalov, Kristin A. Sherry, Jason Romano, Patrick Tinney and Darrell Amy. You all told me writing a book was hard. You all took time to help me with the process. This doesn't happen without you. Thank you all so very much. You are all incredible people.

*Jason Romano, Author of *Live to Forgive* and *The Uniform of Leadership*. Thank you for letting me text you and pick your brain on book writing and podcasting. You are an incredible resource and I am grateful for your friendship. What you're doing is remarkable and I'm honored to call you friend. Thank you for your giving example.

*My Beta Reader team: Donna Harris, Dustin Hall, Aaron Kuchirka and Kristin A. Sherry, Darrin Wilkes. Thank you for lending your time and talents to make suggestions to make this book better. I appreciate you!

*Blake Binns, Damon Burton, Dale Dupree, Larry Levine, Rein Kansman, Lori Knudsen, Jason Romano, Bob Sager, Kristin Sherry and Brian Willett, my endorsers. You guys are incredible friends and I am so fortunate to know you all. Thank you.

*Other incredible people to thank: Pastor Anthony and Shanna Moss; 4 The Cause (Jarrod Price; Randy Witt; Gary Allmon; Jack Halchak); Harry Dennery; Mike White; Larry Lawrence; Tom Roten; David Riedel; Dale and Stephanie Scragg; Demetrius Apostolon; Mike Greene; David Spencer, Jr.; Julie, Delaney and McKenna Bronosky; Matt Gast; Joe Romzek; Joe Leonhardt; Laura Jones; Shad, Dathan and Gabe Holley; Barbara Mathews Hall; Ernie Hargis; Jon Dingledine; Brent Conkright; Bob and Debbie Kitchen; Pastor Mike and Linda Ansell; Johnny and Valerie Riddle and the congregation of New Covenant Pentecostal Church, Chesapeake, Ohio; Pastor David Fairburn and the countless others that impacted mine and my Dad's life over the years.

# ABOUT THE AUTHOR

Brian Sexton is a seasoned veteran Sales, Sales Management, Territory Building and Customer Engagement Specialist of 25 years across four different industries. In his career, Brian has won numerous and has been nominated for Sales awards and set Sales records in his previous companies still unmatched.

Brian has built and managed Sales Territories from $2 to $25 Million in Annual Revenue and is recognized as a People-first leader. Brian is the husband of 24 years to his wife, Tonya and is the father of a son, Bryce, a student at Marshall University. Brian is a minister, singer, musician and the host of The Intentional Encourager Podcast, a podcast releasing twice weekly, a part-time Guest-host and broadcaster for iHeart Media in Huntington, WV and the Voice of the Calvary Baptist Academy Patriots Boys' Basketball program in Hurricane, WV.

# Foreword

Let me be real for a minute. I am not your typical foreword writer. I am a dude who is incredibly passionate about relationships and pouring into others to make them better people. I learned that from my Dad, the late Curtis Dupree. To me, carrying on his legacy is one of the greatest joys in my life, behind being a husband and father. The impact that a father can have on a son is massive. I know this by being a father myself to a young son who will never know his incredible grandfather.

In the Spring of 2018, I first met Brian Sexton on LinkedIn through posts I made about selling copiers and being known as "The Copier Warrior." I've always been intentional about connecting specifically with my audience both in my Sales career and in my Professional online platforms. Connecting with resonance is what my goal is each time I post. Brian shared some comments and frankly, I didn't think much about them. I appreciated them, but I didn't know the guy behind them. What I began to notice, though, was Brian's intentionality and desire to build stronger connections stronger and not be someone else in my network. Brian continued commenting from time to time on posts and again, nothing happened.

I believe, though, God puts people in your path at the right times in life because His timing is always perfect. Fast forward to 2019. I posted on sentiments about my Father and his impact on my life, not only during his time on this earth but also in his absence. My father was an impact-maker, not only on me, but others in our community and industry. To me, Dad was legendary then and is still.

Brian sensed that and immediately reached out to discuss how much his Dad, Jerry Sexton, meant to him and how we shared a common thread in losing them. As a man, son, husband and father, if anyone knew the pain of losing the greatest and most impactful man of my lifetime, it was Brian. The same thing happened to him. There was powerful connection. I knew from the moment I met Brian that we were bonded as brothers, not only from shared experience, but also in Christ. Since that first encounter, Brian has consistently shown up in the relationship he intentionally built between us. He reaches out often simply to encourage me.

Brian is a man of integrity, Faith, compassion, and one of the loudest dudes I have ever met. There is no better person to write about the power of connection than Brian, in my humble opinion. Relationships are the cornerstone of human connection and the reason our lives are abundant with joy and fulfillment. That was the legacy my Dad left and the legacy I live and transmit through The Sales Rebellion. It's uncommon, even rebellious, to desire to build lasting relationships through connection, when society bombards us with instant gratification. True connecting is rebellious behavior.

It's the power of community that shapes impact in our lives. Cultivating communities that thrives on transparency, authenticity, and connecting leaves legacies that moves mountains and resonates through future generations. How we teach our children to connect will be the way they teach their children to connect. How Business leaders and Sales people connect with Internal customers will be flow directly in connection with External customers and truly show the heartbeat of the business. How ministers, counselors, teachers—anyone directly dealing with people on a daily basis—connect with purpose will affect our culture and society far more than elections and policies.

*People Buy From People* goes beyond teaching tricks and tips on being personable and build relationships. That's not who Brian is as an author and as my friend. Brian seeks to challenge preconceived connecting thoughts and ties it directly to the legacy we leave behind and how to progress it for the betterment of our fellow man. Talking heads seek to convince people that somehow the only thing that truly matters are Transactional relationships. The truth is, people desire lasting connection with those they like and trust. Brian brings the focus back to people and the importance of relationships—the way our dads taught us.

As you read this book, you'll understand why Brian and I are the way we are. We are shaped by men who not only believed in connection with every fiber of their beings, they lived it intentionally day after day. I can't think of a better way for a son to honor his late father and leave powerful lessons that will help anyone be a better connector than *People Buy From People*. As you read it, my prayer is that it impacts the way you connect with everyone from family to friends to co-workers and in Professional networks. It's the way Curtis Dupree and Jerry Sexton would connect with you and the way I seek to connect each day I live.

**--Dale Dupree, Leader of The Sales Rebellion**

# INTRODUCTION

We all know people who have "people skills." They possess a natural way of influencing people and a unique ability to convince certain behaviors or thoughts. Some say its charisma, charm or persuasion. Those people understand how to effectively be likeable, trustworthy and relatable. Great leaders are great "people persons." Coaches have an acumen to persuade talented (and sometimes not so talented) athletes to perform to greater levels of success. Ministers and Orators have the ability to move the hearts of people with stirring messages. Public speakers have the ability to connect with audiences all over the world. All these possess the same trait, connection. Great connectors communicate on deep levels making complex ideas very simple. They make unfathomable demands seem palatable and relate to people by being relatable. They talk about things others care deeply about and listen with great intent. They find simple things to start in-depth conversations with others to build life-long relationships. They take life experiences and use them to communicate and connect with equality.

My Dad, Jerry Sexton, was the greatest connector I've known and to countless others that knew him. His 59 years were full of life and love in people he touched and impacted. He was a walking rolodex and knew people I never dreamed he knew. He loved connecting with people and they loved connecting with him. My Dad imparted the book title to me as I left college to begin full-time work in Sales. I remember the conversation from July 1995 as it were yesterday. It's a mantra that has remained with me in my 25 years of Sales, Sales Management and Customer Engagement, and a philosophy I continue to pass on to others. Dad died December 6, 2012, but his words live in this book. He understood connecting skills are made and crafted in conversations by listening, caring and understanding.

In this book, I will share the 10 greatest people lessons Dad used every day. Anyone can use them. These skills make people become better spouses, parents, children (yes, adults can be better children), employees, leaders, friends and mentors. Every day we sell a thought, idea, concept, strategy or connection with us. We want buy-in. We may want our child to clean their room. We may want our team to start turning in reports on time. We want our spouse to be more affectionate. We may want to begin our build a relationship. People respond to people. To get better responses, we must understand how and why people buy from people. It takes time to implement these skills. Here's the good news. We already possess them but don't realize it. When we understand how to take relationships to the next level, we are powerful people. Some believe it's hard to connect with people they have nothing in common. It would be easier, in their minds, for a camel to pass through the eye of a sewing needle, as the Bible teaches. By understanding these 10 lessons and how they really work, it's far easier than camel and needle.

I'd like to say everything in this book is original to me. It isn't. I am merely a facilitator. While my own experience helped shaped these lessons, Dad practiced each one uniquely and was my example to replicate and pass them on to others. Dad truly valued people and relationships. I hope this book will be a conversation between us to understand the person that inspired me to write it. These are truths I was smart enough to implement. Through the 10 chapters, we tackle a topic and look at five truths to consider around it. My desire is to show the kind of buy-in gained to connect with people on a deeper, more fulfilling, substantive level. Dad taught and showed me the key to life was connection. My goal is that people connect better than ever. Connecting allowed Dad to go places he'd never been and see things he'd never seen. At his memorial, over 500 people packed a Funeral-home chapel to show the impact of his connection to them. Connecting has done that for me and so much more. Come with me on a journey to better connection, interaction and relationships with purpose. "Never forget, people buy from people."

"I've learned as much from people what not to do as I've learned from people what to do."
*Jerry D. Sexton*
*1953-2012*

# CHAPTER 1

## *People Buy Consistency*

D ad was a master Consistency creator. Working together, I watched daily for three months the consistent ways he connected. Creating a repeatable, valuable experience for others was incredibly important. In Sales, consistency was his Calling card. If he couldn't create consistent interactions with customers, he believed they wouldn't buy from him. People crave consistency. Like Dad, I'm a creature of habit. Dad had a habit of nicknaming people. I do the same. Until the day he died, every time he answered my call, it was, "HELLO BUCK," my Childhood nickname. As important as creating camaraderie and rapport is creating consistency. Dad felt the people experience should be the same every time. Nebraska Senator Lincoln Chafee says, "Trust is built with consistency." Dad believed consistent people were trustworthy. People buy from those they trust whether they sold starters or Sunday School attendance. Consistency enforces the trust we build. People don't automatically earn trust "just because" but earned through consistent behavior patterns repeated over time.

In a marriage, the feeling of love happens before the development of trust. Trust is built through consistent conversations, actions, reactions and behavior. The adage tells us trust "takes a lifetime to build and a second to destroy." It's only achievable through consistency. While its foundation is repeatable patterns, consistency stands when behaviors change. Kim Garst, Author of "Will the Real You Please Stand Up..." says, "My name is CONSISTENCY. I am related to SUCCESS. We should hang out more often than occasionally." Every successful relationship is consistent. That shouldn't be hard to understand. It's far more important than extolling the virtues of ensuring someone feels good, rather building consistent, lasting relationships. Consistency doesn't desire to be a dominant personality trait. It wants to show up every day, day after day. By mastering consistency in connecting, we ensure successful relationships. Consistency is Time-tested, working yesterday, today, tomorrow and long into the future. By implement and practicing consistency with others, consistency lives well after we're gone. It's that important.

Let's begin by considering consistency in connection.

## CONNECT INSANELY CONSISTENTLY.

As a teenager, Dad made me mow grass to help around the house. He was preparing me to have my own home and mow my own grass. At our house, we had a top yard that sloped to a steep bank leading to flat ground next to the tree-lined bank of the Ohio River. Dad mowed the top and bottom with a riding lawn mower. I had to mow the embankment with a push lawn mower. Dad cautioned me to take it slow and not get my feet close to the mower. Dad saw his brother lose half of a Big toe to a lawn mower. I dreaded starting the mower. A push mower has a rope pulled to instigate a start. It wasn't like Dad's mower, which started by turning a key and begin mowing. Many times, I pulled several times just to achieve a start. It was insane. I had to keep pulling the string and do this every time before mowing. Insanity is defined as doing the same thing repeatedly and expecting a different result. Like starting the mower, each pull of the rope either leads to a start, the desired result, or nothing. If nothing, we pull until achieving a connection inside the small engine of the mower that starts it.

The process, insane as it sounds, doesn't happen without pulling the rope.

At times, starting connections feels like insanity. We repeat the process over and over to get the connection running. Is it the way we're pulling or did we prime the connection correctly? Sometimes connections just don't happen. We may have the greatest people skills and be the nicest, most sincere, honest, caring person on the planet but connection doesn't happen. So, why keep pulling the connecting string? That's insane, right? It's about building consistency. A strong desire to connect feels like insanity due to the resistance of others, but, it's strong desire to be consistent that pushes us to connect consistently. There are times we connect with inconsistent people. People have quirks and layers to their personality uncovered in certain situations and places. It doesn't mean we're inconsistent with them. Consistent connectors make everyone feel important and realize all people have a strong desire to feel consistently important.

People flock to consistency. Successful restaurants are incredibly consistent with food and service. They resist pressure to attempt the latest food trends, opting to add items that remain congruent with a consistent mission. Insane consistency allows those restaurants to have sustainable success. Diners know exactly how the meal tastes before they eat. We should make every encounter consistent. Delivering consistent interactions always leaves people satisfied. Anything else is insanity. Great restaurants resist pressures to "keep things interesting." We may feel pressure to mix it up to keep things fresh, especially in a long-term relationship and fear some relationships finding us stale due to our consistency. Are we still exciting, offering value and giving the very things that drew those connections to us? If we aren't careful, that question can haunt us and tap into our own connecting insanity. Resist the temptation of "spicing things up."

Embrace consistency. Be comfortable with it even when people are uncomfortable with it. Motivational guru, author and speaker, Tony Robbins says this: "It's not what we do occasionally that shapes our lives. It's what we do consistently." Don't look at consistency as insanity. Every interaction shouldn't be an exercise in keeping things lively, but, builds a consistent trust pattern that lasts. Inconsistent people constantly change things up to attract others. They're uncomfortable with consistency and uncomfortable around unconventional people. What is said about people that are vastly different in behaviors and habits? They're insane. Think about it. Haven't we described someone like that who does things that defies our logic? Sure, we have.

We should be so consistent with people that others shake their heads and mutter the same thing...that's INSANE! Those that bedrock on consistency will never feel the urge to change to produce better results. Don't become New Coke. New Coke was overwhelmingly rejected. It wasn't the consistent taste people craved. Be original Coke...The Real Thing. Don't do the insane thing and forget consistency. Consistency makes us unique and develops a thirst in others to model for generations to come. Develop consistency with others and avoid connecting insanity. It's insane and not mundane to connect any other way!

---

### CONNECTING CONCEPTS

➢ **Make eye contact in every interaction**--Eye contact is a powerful way to connect.
➢ **Use the other person's name (or nickname) often**--People love the sound of their own name.
➢ **Repeat back key things said**--This shows sincere listening interest.

---

## DESIRE THE MUNDANE.

Society has a problem with boring. Most believe excitement must be generated or created. Content is king and producing it consistently is hard. We seek to connect with exciting influencers doing big things. Social media positions in companies exist to create buzz and influence decision making. Buzz fades quickly. It's easier creating buzz than building consistency. Dad wasn't boring. He talked to anyone about anything. Dad never talked about anything to create buzz. His conversations centered around topics important to others. In his Sales life, some customers wanted to talk about mundane things and Dad willingly engaged them. Dad didn't like NASCAR. To him, that was boring. Yet, if NASCAR was important to the customer, Dad talked NASCAR. We don't have to love what our connections love but because it's important, we discuss it, even if it bores us to tears. That's real buzz.

Think about buzz. Buzz is the sound a bee makes as it flies. Bees exist to find flowers, pollinate them and collect materials from the flowers the hive needs to produce honey. We don't think about what the bee does, we see the flight and hear the buzz. The bee doesn't exist simply to buzz but connects what the flower needs with what the hive needs. If we connect for the sake of buzz, does anything grow? Creating buzz focuses on the sound and action of drawing people to the noise. Don't rely so heavily on the buzz of collecting and forget that the real purpose is the giving. Buzz only lasts for a moment. Teresa R. Funke, Author of the Bursts of Brilliance for a Creative Life blog says this: "It's ever so fun and fulfilling to be clever, but more lasting and effective to be consistent." The mundane tasks that create consistently don't create the same buzz, but are necessary. Where others around us feel, hear and see the buzz from us is when they experience it consistently. That's the real value of buzz. Something exciting is happening.

Resist the noise that consistency isn't buzzworthy. In the mundane of consistency lurks the temptation to create variety. Doug Cooper, Author of "Outside In" says, "Variety may be the spice of life, but consistency pays the bills." If variety truly is the Spice of life, why do people stick to spices they know best? The right spices add consistent flavor. Consistency pays off. Consistent people resist radical change because it messes with their consistency. Change is good. There are times in life we need change. Abandoning how we consistently interact just to spice things up tastes horrible to others.

5

Tweaking how we connect, though, leads to the right consistent, repeatable recipe every time. When Harlan Sanders (an Honorary Kentucky Colonel) started making fried chicken, the legendary 11 herbs and spices came from trial and error. It was working with the mundane task of seasoning, flouring and frying until the recipe came together. Consistent spices always know how to pair well. One spice may be bold and the other dull, but together, they are scintillating.

Forsaking seemingly mundane truths of consistent interactions doesn't mix well with the expectations of others. Consistency doesn't seem exciting, but it's the healthy way to sustain lasting relationships. When my wife, Tonya, was pregnant with our son, she LOST 30 pounds by consistently eating different foods high in Folic acid. She read that Folic acid was good for brain development and bought in on eating those foods. It worked. Bryce is really smart. Her consistent, mundane food choices turned pregnant cravings into Mind-making meals. We fixate on the mundane when considering how it affects others. When we understand people crave consistent interactions, we tailor their experience to those expectations. It may be dull on the surface, but don't change the mundane.

Don't connect differently to conform to norms. Resist the mindset of being uninteresting. Relationships demand consistency. When things are consistent, people are excited for those interactions. Own a car that's hard to start. It may look good on the outside, but there's problems under the hood that causes inconsistency of starting. The car is supposed to start the same way each time. We count on this basic function. When we connect inconsistently, people are frustrated. They count on consistency. By connecting with seemingly mundane habits, we demonstrate beautiful consistency that eliminates frustration. Show everyone that mundane is marvelous. Every connection is precious. What's mundane to us is precious to them.

The mundane becomes magical and the routine becomes riveting!

---

## CONNECTING CONCEPTS

➤ **Always stay actively engaged in conversation--**
Show value to the passion the other person displays
even in the most mundane of topics.

➤ **Care about the person more than the perspective-**
-Value the person sharing over individual thoughts
on a topic.

➤ **Learn something new about something old-**
-Continue to be informed about topics more
important to others.

---

# LOVE THE ROUTINE.

People are creatures of habit. Everyone has routines or common patterns for starting each day. Get up, go make coffee and breakfast, brush their teeth, take a shower, get dressed, check email, check Social media and off to work. Altering routines can affect one's psyche. Routines don't just appear out of thin air and magically stick. They're designed, thought out, tried and implemented for convenience and efficiency. I learned the value of routine from Dad. In his Sales career, Dad believed customers connected with routine. He saw customers at the same times each month and knew their routines of buying. As a Pastor, Dad always started church at a scheduled time. When I ministered there, he called me in route from my church to his to ensure my timely arrival. He believed in waking up at the same time each morning and believed routines developed consistency. Dad valued consistent people.

Consistent people aren't routine people. They're different. Dad also believed in being different and instilled that in me. It's not routine to do the same thing consistently for people we care about impacting with consistency. In developing routine, some habits are tweaked and new habits formed. The hardest routine I developed was daily prayer. I've been a Christian since age eight. Over my life, though, I haven't prayed daily consistently. A few years ago, I felt an urging from the Lord to begin each day with 30 minutes of prayer. On the first day, I fell asleep about 15 minutes in. I thought, how was I going to do this every morning? Grace. I knew there'd be mornings of falling asleep but I was developing a new routine that needed time. I settled into a great routine that changed my life. Consistency does that. Routines add discipline to daily life. Routines consist of tasks we have to do. Yet, we don't appreciate the consistent behaviors we create with things we have to do. Connecting is similar. We may interact with others routinely, but how do we keep routine interactions interesting? By understanding what others appreciate and expect.

As an 11-year old playing Little League baseball, Dad and coaches had a brainstorm. They changed the way I played baseball through High school. "Buckie has a good arm. We need pitchers. Let's teach Buckie to pitch." One of my coaches taught me a pitching motion and the mechanics of throwing a baseball to my catcher with the goal of consistently hitting the Strike zone. The more I threw, the better I became. Dad, who was my catcher at home, honed my delivery and developed a routine where I pitched consistently well in games. My talent was there, but any success achieved needed consistency. People are wired the same way. They desire consistent interactions that routinely deliver. Effective communication takes mastering a repeatable delivery to others.

Great athletes don't just show up and give a great performance. They work on repetitive consistency. They're laser-focused ensuring every movement is as consistent as the last. This applies to connecting as well. Are we routinely working on connecting, listening and need discovery in every interaction? When we practice those routine connection skills needed, they'll be sharp and repeatable. Hall of Fame pitcher Tom Seaver said this: "In baseball, my theory is to strive for consistency, not to worry about the numbers. If you dwell on statistics, you get shortsighted. If you aim for consistency, the numbers will be there at the end." Most tend to focus on their numbers of connections and not the work of consistent connection.

Without a repeatable delivery of quality interactions, numbers built evaporate quickly. Consistent, well-executed routines are powerful and flawless in connecting with people.

Make it a daily habit to work on the delivery. I can still execute my pitching motion some 38 years later after learning it. It doesn't go away. Great connectors repeat a consistent, routine interaction flawlessly for decades. It's connecting muscle memory and continues drawing people. When people believe with every interaction, they'll receive something consistent, they'll routinely desire more interactions. People are comforted knowing they'll be greeted routinely consistent. A smile, handshake, hug (if proper) or touch of the shoulder (again, if proper) is far less routine today than in times past. Routine interactions delivered consistently last longer than words spoken in them. Repeat that feeling every time for everyone consistently. Key phrasing makes each interaction far from monotonous and makes us anything but a routine connection.

---

## CONNECTING CONCEPTS

➢ **Address people consistently each time**--Be consistent in face-to-face, virtual, email or phone conversations.

➢ **Begin each interaction differently**--"I've been looking forward to talking with you." Or, "The last time we spoke, I had such a great time."

➢ **Each person connects differently**--Understand how they like interactions.

---

## MASTER THE MONOTONOUS.

Hunting is monotonous...so I've heard. Dad didn't hunt. Too boring for him. Waiting for prey to come into view to become food, a mount or both wasn't exciting to Dad. He needed action and typically, that came with a ball, not a gun. Hunters prepare monotonously for a single shot at the prey. Tedious, boring steps to take that perfect shot. Hunters loves the monotonous process of the hunt. When they see what they've been waiting all day for to come into view, the adrenaline rush is exhilarating. Taking the shot and making the shot count is thrilling. We can hunt incredible connections by focusing on the monotonous. Life can be boring. Breathing isn't exciting. It's monotonous, but we die without breath.

We can feel we're dying with connections by believing consistent interactions bore them to death. A fallacy is that consistency is boring, tedious and monotonous. Israelmore Ayivor, Author of Let's Go to the Next Level says: "Consistency is the belt that fastens excellence in position. If you don't do it repeatedly, you'll not excel in it." Putting on a belt is monotonous, but does an incredibly important job keeping our pants from falling. The monotonous, consistent ways we connect with people supports rock-solid connections. Consistency isn't exciting and isn't tedious when it yields fantastic results.

The most monotonous ways people connect are Phone calls and Emails. The last thing many want to do professionally or personally is communicate with those methods when a text or tweet will do. Some aren't excited about sending Emails or connecting by phone. Most enjoy being in front of others who engage with them. In business, ministry or in personal relationships, Phone calls and emails are a Dress rehearsal to the Live performance. Interaction, in any format, can be just as powerful as it is face-to-face. In today's culture, the Virtual meeting has become the method of choice for interpersonal interactions. Every conversation thought to be monotonous in method must be consistent in delivery.

Clear, concise communication signals the ultimate respect for others and keeps us keenly aware of each word's importance. Through perceived monotony, we develop consistency in messaging, connection and ability to replicate important details every time that are far from boring to others. Why do we sometimes feel boredom in tedious tasks? We tend to begin with the beginning in mind. We feel we must craft the perfect interaction to create excitement in it. When we ask for something that needs done, we have the results in mind. Asking is tedious. We begin with the ask, work the other person through our expectations, answer any questions and empower them to the point of completion. Developing consistent connecting habits can take us to any point in the process seamlessly. Being comfortable in the consistent is far from boring. Delivering consistent interactions means being completely in control and in the moment. Monotony becomes magic.

Magical connectors respond routinely and move interactions forward with precision and to Stephen Covey's legendary habit, have the end in mind. By practicing consistent repetition, we're calm, cool, collected and on point. With our seemingly boring consistency we are WINNING! We achieve great interactions! While some are building platforms, we're building people. A consistent approach to connecting isn't monotonous, it's brilliant. When people experience the consistent interactions we deliver, they're never bored. We must guard the against thinking that monotony is boring. People value consistent people. Many Unconventional interactions without consistency leave others unsatisfied and used. Those people choose electricity over consistency. Meanwhile, monotonous, tedious connectors continue consistent interactions others count on consistently. In the story of the Tortoise and the Hare, the monotonous, consistent Tortoise wins the race every time. Create real, consistent value from the monotony. Valuing others means connecting like no other. Don't defend tedious connection. Embrace it.

## CONNECTING CONCEPTS

➤ **Set the stage every time**--People expect the same interactions time and again.
➤ **Use the same phrasing and connecting words**--People feel a kinship to words that build connection.
➤ **Deploy connecting skill effectively and seamlessly**--Resist forcing skills into conversation only for deployment.

## UNCOVER THE UNDERVALUED.

Dad consistently worked to demonstrate the value of every relationship to him. I witnessed a powerful display of a valued friendship. One week before he passed, Dad attended the Funeral service of the wife of his 40-year friend, Ron. I had known Ron all my life and attended church with him at the time. After Ron's wife passed, he asked me to have Dad come to the funeral. Dad agreed to come. I was assisting Ron's family at the service and saw Dad walk in, waiting in the Receiving line. When Dad passed by the casket, he paid his respects to Ron's family and then, Ron. Dad and Ron hugged in a moving moment of genuine embrace. For many years, Dad visited Ron when working in the area of the Daycare center Ron oversaw. Dad loved Ron dearly and demonstrated in the embrace the true value of Ron's friendship.

A week later, I called Ron to tell him of Dad's passing. He was the first person I talked with outside my family that morning. Ron was devastated and was one of the first ones present at Dad's service. Several months passed and Mom attended church with us one Sunday. Ron greeted Mom, asked how she was doing and talked with her for 20-30 minutes. They exchanged phone numbers and talked more. Nine months after my Dad's passing, Ron married Mom. Ron still talks glowingly with me about Dad. He cherishes the value Dad created with their friendship and wants to keep it alive. Value has become an over-cliched word. Everyone defines value differently. Ask Ron about Dad. He knows exactly the value of Dad's friendship and the consistency Dad showed in every interaction.

Most people cannot define the value of consistency. Dad could. He loved consistency and treating people consistently. Most believe consistency is doing the same thing, the same way over and over but don't understand its incredible value. In his Sales role, Dad believed customers not only valued consistency, they craved it and quantified it in dollars. In his Pastoral role, Dad believed consistency led to a greater walk with God and the eternal component at stake applying it daily. In networking, many believe add connections consistently makes them more valuable. Do the number of employees led make a better leader? Do more customers make a better company? Is a bigger church a better church? Perceived outward gratification doesn't ensure internal value created. Real value is doing the same things consistently earning the right to continue stable, lasting relationships. The ability to repeat consistent interactions transfers defined value to others repeatedly. Edmond Mbiaka says, "Actions become very effective when they meet the habit of consistency."

Understanding how people connect and interact with consistent habits, actions and patterns, makes us valuable. Inspirational author, Shannon L. Alder, says this. "Your true power is not in your difference, but in your consistency of being different. The world will always adjust to consistency yet struggle with change." People value consistent connection and want connections that won't surprise them. Don't make it complicated, make it consistent. Consistency valued is consistency reciprocated. That's hard to ignore and impossible to replace. Osho Samuel Adetunji said this. "If you can strike the chord of consistency on the guitar of life, the world will dance to your music of greatness." By valuing consistency, it will take us to unimagined places with incredible people. Prioritize bringing consistent value into every relationship.

Consistent connection is crucial to create constant continuity in every part of life.

---

## CONNECTING CONCEPTS

➤ **Give something specific**--Each interaction is waiting for defined value to be interjected.

➤ **Give more value than expected**--Leave each interaction better than it started.

➤ **Value and reinforce the other person's every word**--People want to feel they are giving value in an interaction as well.

---

**Dad at his church, New Covenant Church, Chesapeake, Ohio, Pastor Appreciation Day, October 2010**

# CHAPTER 2

## *People Buy Thankfulness*

D ad was an incredible gratitude giver in every relationship. Foremost, he was deeply thankful for his relationship with God, Mom, and family. Wonderful relationships aren't by chance. Many relationships he formed I've kept alive. I'm thankful for impactful relationships passed through him to me. How often is "Thank you" said to someone in passing? Likely, more than we realize. Next to "Excuse me" or "I love you," it's a phrase used daily. Do we realize the power of "thank you" and its impact on others? Are we delivering the phrase out of respect or are we truly grateful for a meaningful interaction? In my Sales life, I've gone overboard thanking a customer who bought product. I thought it was what I was supposed to say. Most say "Thank you" only after a transaction. It's proper etiquette. In a professional setting, we don't want to appear unprofessional. It's expected. They're conditioned for the thanks and respond. But, do those words resonate within us? Do we take a moment of gratefulness thanking someone who chooses to interact?

Thinking about thankfulness in every interaction changes the way we connect. Say we meet someone powerful. We may know who they are and what they can do for us. Their connection is life changing. They could greatly enhance our earning power. That's a humbling thought. Immediately, we begin creating the right internal confidence during the interaction that moves to relationship. What if we focused instead on earnest gratitude in those moments? Building earnest gratitude is uncommon and staggering. Adding true, daily thankfulness to every encounter becomes akin to winning the lottery. The results are incredible.

Let's think on thankfulness further.

## DEFER THANKFULLY.

Dad was wonderful at deference. He believed people were to be immediately thanked when doing something and mandated similar behavior from my sister and I. Dad did things for the people in the office who made his job easier. He bought pizzas, gave trinkets and apparel received from vendors or specific items purchased in his travels. By showing deferential gratitude to his internal customers, they moved Heaven and Earth for him. Heaping thanks on those around us is powerfully deferential but being deferential isn't natural. Many have roles in life and business that spotlight them. Maybe they're the point person on a project, lead a Bible study at church, coach a team or lead a department. They take charge and can be a large part of one's psyche. Conventional wisdom teaches the deferential role comes from others. Leaders don't defer, or so we're told.

Deference, in our society, has nearly become extinct and certainly isn't a desirable trait. Social media gives everyone a platform to star in their own show. By posting everything, most don't defer. It becomes boasting rather than deferring. Former University of North Carolina Men's Basketball coach Dean Smith taught his players the ultimate public display of deference. Smith coached players to acknowledge assists in an outward sign of deference by pointing to the passing teammate for the assist after a made basket. Smith wanted his teams to understand that a basket wasn't scored by the scorer without the assist. Most basketball teams of the era didn't do this. Many today still don't, unless they play at UNC, where long-time Coach Roy Williams, who coached under Smith at UNC, still demands the practice of his players. At my son's Alma Mater, the Boy's Head Basketball coach, David Spencer, Jr., shares with every team he coaches ...PREACH. The P stands for, "Point out the assist." Thankful deference at its best.

Deference isn't learned well. From birth, we're conditioned to be selfish and undeferential. Great performers rely on incredible abilities to achieve at high levels and receive accolades for it. When we do things well, we want recognition. We've earned it. Why don't we allow others to enjoy the moment with us? The thankfulness felt about others should be deferred to them in every interaction. It's a prideful thing to realize the impact we make on others when they are thankful. Thankful deference always honors others. Time is a precious gift. Honoring the other person recognizes them for that gift in the interaction. Offering deferential appreciation in that moment sounds like this. "Thank you. I'm grateful and honored for our time together. Thank you for trusting me with it. It's valuable to me. I hope you understand your impact on me and trust I will bring positive impact as well." I can't think of anyone who wouldn't connect with someone so deferential.

Always defer in thankfulness. A thank you to others shouldn't be from what we gained but what they've allowed us to give. Thinking this way enables true appreciation to resonate within us in realization of the power of the relationship. In changing our thinking to reflect on that concept, every interaction changes and flips the script from the rationale dominating our world. A deferential mindset that attracts people. They see it and feel it. It's a powerful way to connect. Great service isn't taught, it's learned and starts with a willingness to do something different. True service is about extraordinary giving to others. Deferring in thankfulness to others makes us heroic connectors. Deference reigns supreme in a grateful, thankful heart and shows others our true selves.

---

## CONNECTING CONCEPTS

➢ **Train the brain to convert "I's" to "We's"**--We includes everyone and excludes no one.
➢ **It's OUR pleasure to serve and defer to others**--Express it in words AND action.
➢ **Create deferential moments of thankfulness**--Lead others introspective thought and deep gratitude.

---

## TOUCH PERSONALLY.

Not long after Dad died, Mom went through his things in stages. The first items Mom gave me were suits, other clothing Dad wore and personal effects. Dad and I were roughly the same size and I began wearing his suits to church. When Mom went through Dad's other things, she called me to her house. Naturally, she was emotional when she called me to come. Mom gave me the watch Dad wore to work every day, a Bible and Preaching notes. The Preaching notes (some in his handwriting) gave me insight to things God gave him that helped those he loved and pastored. I was emotional as I hugged Mom tight and thanked her. It wasn't easy to let those things go. Understandably, there are a few things of Dad's she kept. Mom wasn't passing along stuff, she gave me things important to Dad and knew he'd want me to have them. I cherish these gifts and their importance to me.

There's no feeling quite like receiving a touching gift from someone special. It's like Christmas. When thankfulness truly comes from the heart with sincerity and genuineness from us to others, they feel it. It's hard to ignore deep connection. Some argue that feelings should be kept away from interactions. Absolutely untrue. By transferring a heartfelt thankfulness for the smallest or largest of interactions, we differentiate ourselves. Simply saying "Thank you" isn't enough. Communicating intense gratitude is powerful and heartfelt interaction is impactful. It stirs emotions of respect, joy and humility within us. We transfer that same powerful feeling to others communicating heartfelt thankfulness.

So, what does heartfelt thankfulness look like? It starts on our face. When communicating something heartfelt, make and keep eye contact, soften the voice and choose the right words to express those sentiments. Mumbling or looking away shows disrespect to the other person and their time and makes our words empty. Words not genuinely felt aren't received. Tone is critically important to communicate correctly exactly the way we feel. The tone of words strengthens the emotions behind the words. Words need to line up with action. Gratitude that isn't received in the way we intended or perceived is confusing. "I want them to genuinely know just how much I appreciate them. It's isn't resonating." It's because actions have followed words. Internal conversation should reinforce that principle. The action that lines up with our words is pushing our feelings aside to focus on heartful thankfulness to others. Heartfelt thankfulness is transmitted differently. It's emotional. Allow the action of emotion to align with emotion-filled words and personal touch.

Personal touch adds to the giving of gratitude to others. A handshake, fist-bump, hug or touch is effective reinforcement, but we must know if the receiver is open to it. In a strong relationship, touch cements heartful gratitude. In our church, we hug freely. It demonstrates care. Touch is very powerful in the right setting. We shouldn't become a society that rejects touch or views an ulterior motive when someone touches us or uses a term of endearment. Some terms of endearment are "Honey," "Dear," or Sweetheart." Some use these only when referring to their romantic partner. Others use these to create a non-offensive, home-like feeling. Many from the Baby Boomer generation, like Dad, and those slightly older, use those terms quite a bit, especially at a restaurant in interactions with Wait staff. Personal touch is not to offend or make uncomfortable. Know the audience. It didn't belittle Mom or others or make the Waitress feel uncomfortable, but show heartfelt gratitude for great service. When heartfelt thankfulness is shown in every interaction, people feel at home. Correct personal touch touches people. People truly appreciate heartfelt thankfulness. There's nothing like it.

---

## CONNECTING CONCEPTS

➤ **Check the heart**. Make sure it's seen clearly from the other person's perspective.
➤ **Don't fake heartfelt thankfulness**. If it isn't felt internally, don't express it externally.
➤ **Estimate the receiver.** Express heartfelt thankfulness in ways it impacts them most.

---

## APPRECIATE UNCONDITIONALLY.

As a toddler learning to talk, Dad's older brother, Leroy, would have me say his name and give me a dollar when I said it. Hence, my nickname, Buck. I always said "Thank you." Dad wanted me to understand appreciation when someone extended kindness or gave something of value. True appreciation happens when thanks is given before something is done. The Bible defines this as faith. Faith, in Hebrews 11:1, is defined as, "...the substance of things hoped for and the evidence of things unseen." It's proactive appreciation. We're thankful to God for something good that hasn't happened but believe it will occur. In connection, we typically wait until after an interaction to share heartfelt appreciation. The appreciation is a result of something done for us. When someone grants time to speak with them, do we appreciate on the front end before the conversation begins? It's rare. There doesn't have to be a reason to appreciate others--just appreciate them. Often, the element of surprise triggers the greatest response of true appreciation.

When someone says "Thank you" unconditionally, people are overwhelmed and humbled. That's tremendously powerful. We are incredible connectors when true appreciation for others is engrained in every interaction. How is true appreciation incorporated into every interaction? President John F. Kennedy said this, "As we express our gratitude, we must never forget that the highest appreciation is not to utter words, but to live by them." We incorporate true appreciation by living it. Showing true appreciation to others ratchets up every relationship to new heights. We aren't simply another connection, we're a partner.

When people form Business partnerships, often, the reason is value. One partner has a certain invaluable skill set and teams with people possessing other invaluable skills creating something powerful. Take a Law firm. There may be five Controlling partners in the firm. Each may have a specialty making them the best in their city. Individually, they are great at one specialty of Law. Collectively, they are a powerful firm. We have the ability partnering with others to do incredible things. By showing them true appreciation, they'll conquer worlds with us.

Great connectors are the Gold standard in truly appreciating others. The great Financial planning expert Charles Schwab said, "The best way to develop the best that is in a man (or woman) is by appreciation and encouragement." True appreciation stirs deep, inspirational emotions in people. It makes them feel 10 feet tall. They'll fight, defend and stand with us. Schwab not only built impeccable trust with clients, but also appreciated them like no one else. People kept investing with Schwab and referred him to others. When people feel true appreciation, they tell everyone. While happiness is a vital component to long-term success in any relationship, what people value is appreciation. Connections, customers, church members and friends never leave when they're appreciated. Talk about a comfort zone.

True appreciation leads to unbreakable commitment. To insulate a network from erosion, practice true appreciation with everyone in it. If I want to evoke true appreciation in my wife, I do things around our house before she asks. I won't even tell her I am going to do something; I just do it. She feels relieved, valued and appreciated by doing something she didn't have to do. If we'll do those things for our loved ones, we can also serve others the same way. People love true appreciation and Ddemonstrating it true appreciation bwill becomes a staple of every interaction.

---

## CONNECTING CONCEPTS

➤ **Show true appreciation proactively**--A Social Media post or email to someone close to them personally or professionally resonates.

➤ **Connect people to others with a reason of appreciation**--Show the value and the true appreciation felt for the person we refer.

➤ **Send true appreciation in writing**--Encourage the other person with something they can keep and reference often.

---

## STAPLE CONTINUALLY.

Losing Dad in 2012 was a turning point in my thankfulness. He's not here to tell directly, but I'm more thankful each day for him and his impact on my life. I honor his memory thankfully. Incorporating thankfulness into daily routine leads us to more things to appreciate. A life-altering experience, near-death experience or traumatic life event causes people to look at life much differently. They tend not to be angry over small things and try to be more giving and loving. They appreciate life more and find gratitude in simplicity. It's a new way of living. We can take the same approach without the life-altering event by choosing to make thankfulness a staple of everyday life. Ralph Marston said, "Make it a habit to tell people thank you. To express your appreciation, sincerely and without the expectation of anything in return." What if we implemented thankfulness with every interaction? By making it a staple, it changes everything and shows who we really are. We become known for it. Australian Super model Miranda Kerr says, "I think for any relationship to be successful, there needs to be loving communication, appreciation and understanding."

Beginning interactions with appreciation sets us apart and becomes an expected staple by others. What a powerful way to be defined. Some businesses sell "staple" products customers know they always find. Staples are essential for survival of not only the business, but its customers. Staples are also critical items to have on hand in case of a significant weather emergency that triggers a power outage. In a household, most staples are milk, Bottled water, bread, eggs, paper towels, toilet paper, Cleaning supplies and other items essential to the smooth running of the house. The typical food wants of a household take a backseat to the staples kept on hand. Giving people thankfulness in interactions isn't something we always find ourselves. All the more reason to make it a staple of every interaction.

One of my favorite All-time Television shows is the American version of The Office. For nearly seven seasons, the lead character, Michael Scott (played brilliantly by Steve Carell) was passionate about a staple item, paper. To Michael, paper was his life and the people at Dunder Mifflin, a Paper company, his family. Everything in his world was built around a staple and a staple of Michael's character was the thankfulness, appreciation and palpable love for each of the other characters. Imagine if every interaction was built around the staple of thankfulness? We may have people we've known for many years either in a personal or work relationship. We know how we feel about them and believe we know how they feel about us. However, we will reshape interactions and turn things upside down with true appreciation as a staple.

Consistent, true appreciation makes everyone stand at attention and sends a strong signal to everyone that we practice and embody it. True appreciation creates legendary and irreplaceable people. What if we became irreplaceable to everyone around us and were the talk of our connections? What if everyone saw true appreciation exhibited in us that they'd do anything to connect?

Proactively and truly appreciate and interact like no one else and we'll experience that. When we truly appreciate people, people buy in and experience connection powerfully. True appreciation raises respect to a whole new level and people will love us for it.

---

## CONNECTING CONCEPTS

➢ **Know and express true thankfulness to others--**
They may need to hear it.
➢ **True appreciation should be devoid of fluff--**
Consistently say what we mean and mean what we say.
➢ **Always place utmost importance on others with true appreciation--**Resist the opportunity for credit even when deserved.

---

## LOVE STRONGLY.

Dad's favorite baseball team was the Cincinnati Reds. We both loved the Reds. I've been a Reds fan since I was a kid. They're the only Major League baseball team I care to watch. I care what happens to their health and well-being; if they're on the field. That's my team and always will be. The Reds are the closest MLB team geographically to us, about a three-hour drive west. My area has always been known as "Reds Country." I listening to and watched Reds games with Dad. Dad told me I watched the 1972 World Series between the Reds and the Oakland A's with him as a two-month-old in his arms. My earliest recollection of going to a Reds game was in 1977 as a five-year-old. My Dad created that love of Reds baseball in me. It's amazing how we throw the word love around so easily describing our feelings toward things.

Love is a powerful word. The only woman that I love romantically is my wife of 24 years, Tonya. I wouldn't dare say "I love you" to another woman in that same way. I love my son, Mom,

Mother-in-Law, sisters, Sister-in-Law, nieces, nephews and cousins with a Familial love. I love my Pastor, Church family and close friends with a Familial love as well. It signifies that I'll go to great lengths for them. Love for others is shown in incredible, impactful way and our feelings for them creates deep appreciation for their being a part of our lives. I can't imagine life without my wife and son. They are my world. When we think about the people in our lives closest to us but not family, strong emotion swells within us. We love them not just for what they've done <u>for</u> us but who they are <u>to</u> us. Loving people in that way, we create eternal thankfulness for the impact made in our lives.

When Dad passed away, I became extremely grateful for his impact and the things he imparted to me and taught me. When I visit his grave, I say "Thank you" as well as "I love you." My gratitude comes from strong love and deep respect for the man Dad was and the impact in lives I hope to make. When people see thankfulness from a strong place of love, they respond differently. Loving people is powerful. If we don't love people, they'll leave our lives. I watched Dad love people. Dad looked at people with a true feeling of love, gratitude and respect. I saw it in his eyes. When Dad interacted with people he loved, he was different. I saw it when we worked together and I shared similar feelings with many of my customers in my Sales career. Wonderful gratitude toward others comes from a strong place of love. Many don't spend time getting to know others on deep levels, rather, they pursue a "you scratch my back and I'll scratch yours" relationship. The new Golden Rule is: Do something for others because they've done something for us first.

Love gives before it receives and shares with no thought of return. Love does first before something is done for it. Surprise someone we love with something they love just because. Their response is often unbelievable. Giving gratitude from a strong place of love changes everything. Loving people means we want the absolute best for them. Emotions change when people feel their best interests are truly being valued. Why feel so strongly about loving people? We become transparently honest with others. When there's issues, we proactively share. When others have issues, we proactively listen. Listening from a strong place of love causes us to hear people differently. We hear them from our heart. The heart values people. Connections are not just things we collect. They're valuable. When we're thankful to people from a strong place of love, we're reminded what we cherish about them. We focus on the qualities that bond the relationship, what makes it stronger and things can continue to do to make it better.

To get to better, we have to go through bitter. Bad news is never easy to deliver and delivering it to people we love is painful. However, offering others a solution and reassuring from a strong place of love shows our devotion to them and demonstrates the true gratitude of the relationship. Relationships grow stronger when integrity is demonstrated. A strong place of love fosters integrity. People full of integrity connect powerfully for a lifetime and are never fake. Thankfulness is something you can't fake. People see through artificial gratitude. Real, genuine gratitude is incredible in the mind and soul because it isn't thought about often. Gratitude is reactionary. Buy something and I'll recognize it with canned gratitude. Authentic gratitude is never forced, and fosters a powerful exchange between parties with deep respect for each other. Two of the most powerful words spoken are "Thank you." Say them daily and watch the power they bring.

---

## CONNECTING CONCEPTS

- ➤ **Put love into every interaction**--Smiles, gestures and greetings filled with emotion demonstrate strong love.
- ➤ **Love others when we aren't feeling in in the moment**--Love never goes unnoticed.
- ➤ **Love is reciprocated and felt and when genuine**--Love first without expecting immediate return.

---

Dad and I at a Barboursville, WV restaurant celebrating his 58th birthday, April 2011.

# CHAPTER 3

## *People Buy Empathy*

Life radically changed December 6, 2012. I was in Boone, North Carolina beginning my day of making Sales calls and heading back to West Virginia in time to catch my son's Basketball game. When my sister called me at 6:45 AM, I thought she wanted to tell me something about my nieces. I never dreamed she'd utter the words, "Dad's gone." I talked to Dad at four PM the previous day. This wasn't supposed to happen to MY Dad. He was pastoring a church; we were working together and he had grandkids to be a part of their lives. This WAS NOT HAPPENING! After getting a few details, I dropped the phone on the bed and sobbed uncontrollably. I don't lose it emotionally, but I lost it. My hero was gone.

For the first time in my life, I was heartbroken. At one point, I looked to the ceiling and said, "God, why? We had a plan! We had a plan!" Then, the Lord spoke to my heart and said, "You can praise Me when things are good, but can you praise Me when your world is falling apart?" From that moment on, this was my world. I quickly understood the anguish my wife felt the moment her Dad passed away. Empathy hit me like a ton of bricks. My wife was much more empathetic to me in my time of grief than I was in hers.

Empathy is brilliant in that it forces us to understand what others have gone through before us. Empathy builds connecting bridges.

I've seen situations where connections, customers, family and friends have gone through similar tragedies in their own lives. One customer lost a child nearly eight months into a pregnancy. Another had their adult son choke to death in his Arizona apartment and had to fly his body back to West Virginia. Another lost a teenage son in a four-wheeler accident. I've watched customers lose homes and businesses to fire. Most consider themselves to be empathetic but some are pathetic at empathy. Empathy by the Merriam-Webster definition is "the feeling that you understand another person's experiences and emotions and the ability to share someone else's feelings." I've seen heartache from people I cared for deeply, yet I didn't understand. We've all had similar instances. I had to learn empathy in those situations. I hadn't gone through that type of trial. Life, at times, just sucks.

Empathy allows us to be many things to many people. In business, sometimes, customers don't need a Sales partner, they need a friend. Empathy is more powerful than expertise. Being an understanding voice of reason helps guide people through rough spots. My Pastor, Anthony Moss, often says, "People don't care how much you know until they know how much you care." Sharing a similar life experience in the right moment is salve to sooth a deep emotional wound. It doesn't have to be profound wisdom, rather the right words shared empathetically. In those emotional moments, understand, help and empathize.

Let's explore the ways empathy connects exceptionally.

## PUNT AWAY PITY.

Growing up, Dad didn't have much pity on us. When my sister or I would scrape a knee, fall and hurt ourselves and cry, he'd say, "Dry it up." The same rule went for playing wiffleball in the yard with him or during a spanking. Dad had little pity on what he felt was small pain. This changed DRASTICALLY when he had grandchildren. If they cried, Pap picked them up and tried soothing their hurt little body and spirit. As a teenager, we watched a TV show called, "The A-Team." Dad and I both liked the show. My favorite character was B.A. Barracus, played by Mr. T. A line delivered in every episode by Barracus would be, "Shut up, Fool!" In 2006, some 24 years after Mr. T. played in the A-Team, TV Land produced and aired a series starring him called "I Pity the Fool." The premise of the show would be a kinder, gentler Mr. T., traveling from city to city problem solving and giving life advice. Mr. T. saw pity as a dangerous thing.

Pity's danger is destroying confidence, killing courage and hating hope. Pity desires three C's: comfort, company and coddling. Pity thinks because its miserable, everyone should be miserable. Pity is selfish and doesn't care about happiness. Pity's job is to make everyone uncomfortable. Some see pity and want to remove the problem instead of lifting the person. Pity causes us to see people through skewed lenses. We see flaws over flawlessness. Many don't want pity; they want a different situation. Everyone faces challenges, in business, in Sales, in leadership and life. The economy is bad. Sales are down. People have mistreated them. They can't please anyone. Multitudes have come through pitiful circumstances. Multitudes more have overcome. Encourage overcoming behavior. Some love pity parties. In life, we get invited to lots of Pity parties. We throw them ourselves from time to time. Bringing a gift called empathy to the pity party, however, turns it around. How? Empathy thrives in understanding. By understanding why someone is in a situation, we can offer a solution. By not recognizing pity, we give a hand up rather than a handout. Party on!

We're all one life-changing negative event from pitiful. Hope to a person in a pitiful situation is powerful. Hope is its own celebration. Showing and telling someone things will be okay is more than okay. The natural reaction is to hand hold and offer a shoulder to cry on, soothing the situation for the moment. When the moment is gone, the problem remains. Empathy sees past the situation. Yes, it's raining but not forever. The sun comes up tomorrow. It usually does. Don't feel the need to have all the answers in a tough situation. Steer thinking towards the positives of the future instead of the reality of the present. Offer something hopeful that could turn things around. Stephen Covey says, "Seek to understand, then be understood." Understand that people in desperate situations will cling to anything that will get them out.

Never overpromise hope. Encourage. Enlighten. Empathize. We can speak life to the pitiful. When we empathize, we transmit powerful solutions to pitiful circumstances. Empathy puts us in a place of taking charge and putting pity in its rightful place...out the door. By helping others see a new day dawning, we transform pity into positivity. By puntingtting away pity, we become favorable connectors, powerful, strong and impactful.

---

## CONNECTING CONCEPTS

➢ **Give forward-thinking responses**--Pity can't stay in the midst of a positive decided answer.
➢ **Don't dwell in uncertainties**--Offer certain responses to uncertain questions.
➢ **Use intentional empathy**--Speak directly to the situation, not around it.

---

## FAVOR OTHERS FAVORABLY.

I smile when hearing the phrase, "First-world problems." It reminds me when Dad got an iPhone. As he began using it, he was frustrated. There weren't actual buttons to push on the phone as he was accustomed. He wasn't interested in surfing the Web, using Maps or any of the countless apps. He wanted to dial a number, talk and send the occasional text. Eventually, he gave the phone to my sister. I already had an iPhone and loved it and was dumbfounded why he didn't. We have issues that most of the world would give anything to experience. We complain when the power goes out during a storm, the air conditioner stops working or our cell phone is too slow. Many across the globe don't have homes, air conditioning or phones. They struggle to have clean drinking water and food. We don't understand those problems because we don't have them. It's hard wrapping our minds around what some do to survive.

Things don't move our emotions like they used to move them. We overlook the problems of others and it seems we've forgotten how to care for our fellow man. Now, many say, "Why won't someone help me?" We have become a society of Emotional Support dogs, soothing Baby dolls to help our stress levels and other "support tools" instead of dealing with our problems. We are keenly self-aware about things that attack our paychecks, snarky posts and thinking someone is getting something we aren't. We're a selfish society. Here's an idea. Let's be people more interested in giving and finding out what's most important to others. Invest greater in people than things.

As a parent, I want to invest in how my son thinks and reacts in certain situations. How would he handle adversity? How would he handle great success? How would he react to being accused of something he didn't do? How would he protect his family? In life, we try to understand people going through those very things. Success is incredible, but it can be scary. Helping others provides the confidence they need to handle those situations accordingly. It's the greatest favor we extend to others. People want to know they have the confidence of others and confidently favoring others helps them exude confidence. It's calculated and exactly what's needed to best help that person succeed. Favoring others and having their best interests in mind, demonstrates the value people bring in every situation. If I offered someone a million dollars, but insisted for them to have it, I'd need half, how would it favor them? It doesn't. They should get the full million. Don't let selfishness stand in the way of favoring others in interactions. No one benefits.

When asked to offer a solution to someone, remove the thought of personal benefit. Seek to favor the other person who has thought enough of us to ask. We need more selfless actions and less selfish motives. To have true differentiation in the minds of others is to think and act selflessly. Be the person that changes their world by making others better. When I dated my wife, Tonya, I wanted to make her happy. I took her to restaurants she liked. I wore things she liked on me. I wanted to her to favor me with her love. I wanted to understand what she liked and wanted so I could please her. It was about favoring her.

People love being favored. How do we get someone's attention on their birthday or Christmas? Get them something they want. Favoring others takes finding out exactly what they want, dream and desire. Understanding those things favor people in ways that turn their world upside down. We deliver favor at an untouchable level. Understanding favor towards others deflects any glory to us and reminds us that we're nothing without others.

---

## CONNECTING CONCEPTS

➤ **Serve before being served**--People are blown away when shown great favor.

➤ **Don't favor someone to expect future reciprocity-** -Keep the motives pure.

➤ **Be genuine when favoring others**--A false attitude is easily exposed.

---

## PAT ON THE BACK.

One year during my childhood, our family took a vacation to Beaufort, South Carolina. It was a lovely area and we were excited to be on a trip. I remember walking into an old bookstore with Dad. In this bookstore, I found a 1972 Major League Baseball Media guide. I was in awe flipping through the pages. This was the year I was born. I begged Dad to buy it and he allowed and funded the twenty-five-cent purchase. I read that book so often both paper covers came off. In the book, I remember the profile on Los Angeles Dodgers pitcher, Claude Osteen. His nickname was "Gomer" because he resembled actor Jim Nabors, who played the Gomer Pyle character on television. Osteen was known for one particular colorful quote. "A pat on the back is merely 18 inches from a kick in the butt." Translation: Don't get caught seeking accolades one minute, for the next minute a mistake is apt to come quickly. I've never forgotten that quote. Accolades are fleeting.

Accolades feel good. However, when our minds and hearts aren't in the right place, we find more kicks in the rear than pats on the back. If we're more interested in credit than helping others, it's not a connection problem, it's a heart problem. We've forgotten how to serve. Great connectors always have their people compass pointed in the right direction. They know they aren't the end-all, be-all in the relationship. I've won multiple Selling awards. The last thing I should exude is arrogance. Even if I share a transformative idea that revolutionizes someone's business and brings wealth beyond their wildest dreams, it's not my position to boast. For every successful idea we present, there are times when an idea shared causes a disaster. That's not the time to rest on laurels. We don't take credit but celebrate and share the success.

Celebrations are wonderful. Some celebrate their acumen, experience and expertise and believe that makes them successful. They forget the basics. The day we leave others out of celebrations, we'll celebrate by ourselves. It's not by our greatness people are successful and success doesn't automatically follow us. People won't interact with those who make them feel inferior. Celebrate successes privately and don't celebrate long. Sports Talk Radio host Colin Cowherd says this: "Celebrate rarely." There's still work to do. Stay prepared to help others and celebrate things important to others. In business, being a market expert means staying on top of things solely to help others. Helping customers succeed is a celebration. When others celebrate achievements, our internal satisfaction comes from people we've helped gain external satisfaction. That demonstrates ability and credibility.

Credibility from helping others comes right behind building rapport. When we help others, it's not a Brag session or a

Hall-of-Fame speech. We can provide a list of accomplishments pages long to others and make enough Credibility statements to fill books. If we don't care enough to understand people and what they need from the relationship, we fail. We're the conduit to success, not the power behind it. Without the conduit of humility and the outlet of understanding, we'll never power anything.

There is power in humility with a strong internal sense of our value to others. Yet, we must resist the temptation to constantly take credit when things we say or do impacts people. Let others toot horns and sing praises. While on the topic, let's address something. In a referral-based industry, referrals are gifts. If it's our birthday, we shouldn't have to ask for cake or ice cream. When we do something great for someone, don't ask them to tell others about it. If we serve and care for people impeccably, referrals come as does a well-deserved pat on the back. HBy humbling ourselves and making relationships about others t, we takes interactions to the next level.

---

## CONNECTING CONCEPTS

➢ **Humility is always in order**--When someone heaps praise on us, stay humble.
➢ **Turn the praise back to the other person**--Use the phrasing, "You're too kind. It's because of you."
➢ **Offer a sincere compliment in return of praise**-- "You truly are a joy to know." "You make it so easy to do business with." "You are an incredible giver yourself.

---

## CARE NEXT LEVEL.

Dad always looked to move things to the next level. When we teamed professionally in February 2012, he believed he and I could take the company to the next level. He wanted to establish market domination, pass the torch to me and leave the company at new heights. Each day, we talked about the next level and in our last conversation, we formulated a Next-level idea that never came to fruition. I still wonder what might have been. People dream about taking their talents, current role and abilities to the Next level. Going to the Next level is intimidating. The next level, usually takes a giant leap in the skill, work and effort needed to get and stay there. Taking anything to the Next level requires commitment, sacrifice, dedication and intention. It's hard. We aren't going to wake up at the next level of doing anything. It's extremely intentional. Next-level, intentional empathy is rare but not impossible to use at an Elite level to build intense loyalty in others.

When people see Next-level type of care about them, the wheels turn. In business, treating prospective customers with a next-level care BEFORE they buy makes them wonder what actually buying is like. Next level caring with nothing on the line means continuing that care when dollars are exchanged. Empathy today is transactional. Care first, then I'll care. Next-level empathy leads, never follows, cares first, cares often, finds deeper ways to what matters most to others and cares uncommonly. Here's an example. Let's say someone is passionate about Children's ministries, but we aren't a Christian ourselves. That's tough spot to understand, but not as much of a stretch as one might imagine. Asking questions about the why. Why are Children's ministries so important to them? Why are they involved? Ask questions for understanding. We may not agree their why but we care deeply enough to ask to understand.

Being educated on things important to others is Next-level. Focus interactions on deepening our education. Some use a certain topic as an aside. It isn't the real focus of the discussion. Resist that thinking and understand that every topic in conversation matters. Great connectors use every topic in building connecting structures brick by brick. Caring for people builds lifelong, fulfilling relationships. When every interaction begins around them and things important to them, we operate at the Next level. It's unprecedented. When it's more important that lasting, personal bonds are formed rather than the size of our network, we care at the Next level. To change connecting as we know it, we change the way we care about people. Let's start now caring, sharing and operating empathetically at the Next level. Then, we will be a Next-level unifiers and will always have conversations with people on common ground.

---

## CONNECTING CONCEPTS

> ➤ **Be consistent in the level of caring--**It's powerful when others understand it fully.
> ➤ **Begin conversations around previously discussed topics--**It promotes familiarity and demonstrates superior listening and understanding skills.
> ➤ **Gear more questions around familiar topics--** Continues to demonstrates Next-level empathy and build more knowledge.

---

## EQUALIZE ALL PEOPLE.

I never saw Dad treat anyone unequally. No one was ever beneath him and he believed he was no better than anyone else. He loved people of all races, colors, creeds, origin and sex. I saw Dad love Black people as much as White people. To him, they were just people and it didn't matter to him what they looked like. I feel exactly the same. I have friends of all shapes, sizes, color, race and creed. I treat them all equally. Equality has been a generational term seeking to level an unlevel playing field. Whether speaking of Racial equality or Gender equality, the two most prominent Equality issues in my lifetime, the subject has many layers and has sparked unending debate.

Equality, at times, has been undefinable yet, has functioned beautifully when executed correctly. Equality has led to necessary changes, yet, in many ways, society still has far to go. As the old saying goes, "We all put our pants on the same way, one leg at a time." We are no better than anyone else. As a man, I am not the dominant species. When God created woman from Adam, the first human, He put Adam in a deep sleep and took a rib from him. God could have used anything to create Eve but took the bone closest to Adam's heart to create a woman, that would be his helpmate. When a man takes a wife, they are equal in God's sight. God never intended the woman to be inferior or any race of people to be superior to another.

In my first Sales role at 22, I worked for a legendary man, Harry Dennery. Harry was a brilliant businessman and one of the neatest people I've ever known. Talking with me one day, Harry shared an unforgettable piece of Life advice. "Brian, treat everyone the same. You never know when the Dishwasher will become the Buyer." The value of equality in business is simple. Treat everyone the same. Along with Dad, Harry showed me how to equalize all people. Treat everyone equally every time earns immense respect from others. Caring for everyone equally develops rare camaraderie. In Sales, many treat the Decision-Maker as the star of the show. Those around them become bit players. However, when those we've developed a fantastic relationship leave for a better opportunity (or gets asked to leave), someone else fills the role. Caring for everyone equally insulates us in those situations. Developing incredible relationships with everyone helps overcome any hiccups with potential replacements and build strong bonds. Strong connectors interact the same way with everyone.

Treating everyone equally takes two important skills, watching and listening. Watching what others do and how they do it help us understand what and why they do it. Intent listening focuses us on what is important to others and people view their importance. Yogi Berra, the Hall of Fame Baseball catcher eloquently said it. "You can observe a lot by watching." Observation involves intense listening enabling us to pick up things that are in tune with others. In many concerts, performers have a Live band of some sort playing various instruments. Near the intermission, the performer takes the opportunity for a song or two to feature the band. Great live performers always feature the band. It gives the performer a Vocal break and allows the band to show off their individual and collective talents for the audience. For the bulk of the show, the audience is focused on the headliner. The headliner knows the show wouldn't be worth watching without the talents of the band and introduce the Band members asking for equal appreciation from the audience.

In Sales or Leadership, make sure to feature the band. Make it a point to take a few minutes each day to care equally for those folks who "do the dirty work." Find out what's happening in their life. Don't talk business. Equalize them and treat them like the featured performer. When we show empathy that equalizes all those we touch, we'll be the star everyone wants to see perform. There's nothing in life more powerful than connecting with true empathy. Empathy displayed in connection empowered.

---

## CONNECTING CONCEPTS

- ➢ **Everyone is equal in our eyes**--Avoid the temptation of treating others differently.
- ➢ **Use the same tone, pacing and dialect with others**--Speak as they speak.
- ➢ **Everyone is consistently unique**--Make them feel as though there's no one else in the world like them.

---

Dad singing with my quartet, 4 The Cause, during a 2010 service at his church in Chesapeake, Ohio. (Pictured from left to right: Me, Dad, Jarrod Price, Jack Halchak and Randy Witt.)

# CHAPTER 4

## *People Buy Meekness*

D

ad was intentional that he and Mom raise my sisters and I in church. Church was a vital part of my life growing up. I gave my life to the Lord at nine and began reading and studying the Bible. I have one of Dad's Bibles I use when preaching. My son has the one Dad read most. I developed a love for the Scriptures through Dad's influence. He encouraged me to memorize the Bible. A famous passage of scripture is called The Beatitudes, a series of blessings from The Lord Jesus Christ. A couple of well-known blessings are: "Blessed are they that hunger and thirst after righteousness, for they shall be filled." "Blessed are the pure in heart, for they shall see God." The blessing that fits with this chapter is Verse 5 which says: "Blessed are the meek, for they shall inherit the earth." Meekness isn't a subject often broached. It isn't emphasized in trainings or featured in Mission statements. Meekness isn't something we think about. It's a forgotten character trait. Meekness, as defined by Dictionary.com, is "overly submissive or compliant; tame; humbly patient or docile; as under provocation from others." Meekness, on its own, doesn't "WOW" a crowd.

The point of meekness is to not stand out at all. Meekness is good with no one noticing. Meekness just wants to be, not the end-all be-all. Meekness is best left to be consistent in its operation. Many would rather run from meekness than celebrate it. In business, people don't want to be known as being "overly compliant." Docile? No way. Humbly patient? Most believe they won't survive personally or professionally being humbly patient. It's why many climb the ladder. Meekness isn't something people desire to develop. No one wants to be thought of as "spiritless." For most outgoing personality types, meekness isn't something they desire to exhibit. They'd rather others exhibit that trait. Most people put the extroverted characteristics of their personality in the forefront and let the Expressive side out to play. Meekness wants to stay inside and play to the docile side. The problem most people have with meekness is how and when to use it. It helps in times we need a Reality check.

Meekness is an uncomfortable personality trait. Think about meek people. What characteristics come to mind? Quiet? Shy? Tends to stay in the background? Thoughtful? Unassuming? Many believe meek people have nothing to add and won't possibly bring any value. Most of the time, the meek are the strategic. They won't get caught inserting foot in mouth because they tend to not open their mouths at all. There's likely a time or two in we've had to learn meekness and been in situations where meekness was forced on us. What if we used meekness to its full potential and to our advantage in interactions with others? We'll impact everyone around us by being proactively meek.

Let's move into how to master meekness.

## MAKE "ME" INTENTIONALLY MEEK.

Dad was seemingly always in the spotlight. Growing up, Dad was in the church choir, sang solos and was a Lead singer in a Male Southern Gospel quartet. Not only did he sing, but also played Saxophone. As a minister, Dad became a proficient preacher and teacher. I believe, though, his greatest talent was developing others. I started singing at age three. When my voice changed at 12, Dad started singing in a lower register, so I could sing the part he sang. He didn't have to do that, but it was more important that I develop vocally. He showed meekness during an awkward time for me. Fast forward to 2017. Our quartet lost its baritone singer. I remembered Dad making that move for me and I made the same move to accommodate our new Tenor singer, who sang higher than I. Had Dad not showed meekness and changed parts for me, I wouldn't have seen the best way to make a similar move. Past meekness displayed reminds us how to display it presently.

Meekness doesn't display well in self-absorbed people. Every conversation is about them. Selfies abound in their Social media presence. When it comes to taking credit, they take it and RUN with it! Some people love the spotlight. They love accolades and will do just about anything to get them. Meekness, however, creates a real solace in privacy. Not everyone needs to know our business. Good things should be shared in moderation and with a meek spirit. There is nothing wrong with praise, especially for a job well done. Awards, accolades and honors are great things to do for great performers. If our work is done for praise alone, we need a big shot of meekness. Helping others get precisely what they need and want makes us revolutionarily meek. In my 25-year Sales career, I never saw customers disappointed with humility. We can't do business, relationships or anything on our own. We're not the star of the show. We need people.

When serving others in meekness, we lose ourselves and reject thoughts that want to rise in the moment that we've done something great. Meekness doesn't seek greatness, but values greatness in others. One of the best pieces of advice I received in my career was: "Brian, always be prepared to replace your best customer." Think about people in life we can't afford to lose. How would we react if those people told us they didn't want to be in our lives? We'd be devastated. What did we do wrong? How did this happen? Where did we fail? Now, take the questioning in this direction. What can I do better for important people in my life? How can I show more humility and patience with them? Where can I add more value to them? Have I truly demonstrated how important they are?

Some demonstrate importance as a front to woo people. In our chameleon culture, people hide behind avatars, call themselves different names and do other things hiding who they really are. We should always be our true selves consistently. I strive to be the same person all the time, whether I'm at Walmart, on the job, at church or at home. Some have a certain persona to connect, but act differently once connected. Meekness should be a consistent part of everyday life, not when attracting people. Don't connect for credit, handshakes and pats on the back.

Be intentionally meek toward others. It's about what we give, not what we get. Meek people give so much others feel like the King or Queen of the World. Pour into others so much they're excited to interact. Turn every encounter into a fantastic opportunity for others to be energized and an amazing experience where they are the star. By putting ourselves aside, we win people! Being meek is never confused for being weak.

---

## CONNECTING CONCEPTS

- ➤ **Always accept praise humbly**--Don't dismiss or defer. It insults the other person.
- ➤ **Use facial gestures and greetings that show meekness**--If others are open to an embrace such as a hug or handshake, add eye contact that shows meekness.
- ➤ **Put listening over speaking**--Meek people demonstrate that skill often in interactions.

---

## CONFUSE MEEKNESS FOR WEAKNESS AND CAUSE CONFUSION.

As a kid coming home from church or going to church, Dad and Mom sang a song with me we learned in Sunday School classes called "Jesus Loves Me." I was three the first time I remember singing it. A line in the song still resonates. "Little ones to Him belong; They are weak but He is strong." People don't want to be considered weak. Weak is used in many different applications. "That proposal was <u>WEAK</u>!" "Even though I feel better, I'm still weak." "The market today finished weak as stocks took a momentary downturn over fears of rising Unemployment numbers." Weak isn't something we want to feel, mentally or physically. When looking internally at ourselves, we focus on strengths rather than weaknesses. Weakness shows what we lack, not what we possess. Companies don't hire people for weaknesses displayed, but strengths that will invigorate the organization. When people have clearly defined weaknesses, training is deployed to turn those weaknesses into strengths. It's called "Coaching up."

Most seek coaching when weaknesses are exposed. Few enter any profession with well-rounded skills. Most people have skills that need developing. I've always been strong with people but other weaknesses such as talking too much and not listening enough, turned into strengths with time, training and practice. Intentionally meek leaders pointed out weaknesses in me they coached into strengths. Coaching shouldn't attempt to change personality, but embrace and enhance other behaviors that need developing. Meekness is a concept most leaders don't coach. People considered to be meek are thought to not be aggressive, dynamic or engaging. Nothing could be further from the truth. Desire more meekness and encourage it in others.

Exhibiting meekness has incorrectly been thought to cajole others and letting them walk over us. This is such outdated and Neanderthal-like thinking. People welcome people strong in meekness. If meekness is a weakness, connecting becomes difficult. By using it in the right ways and times, meekness is a strength. In business, meekness isn't morphing into a doormat giving customers everything they want. Meekness listens intently to customers and transforms weak business components into strong ones. Allowing meekness to be a strength transforms everything. People replicate strengths seen in others.

Turning meekness into a strength sets us apart and is a rarely discussed advantage. Why be like everyone else? Meekness, as a strength, allows others relaxed interactions as we connect deferentially. Meekness shows utmost respect as ideas flow back and forth between people instead of one person pitching and the other catching. Arrogant interactions show more interest in pitching and makes others feel inferior. It's a marked weakness. Display meekness and show people a connector that truly cares about them no matter what. Turning meekness into a strength demonstrates being tame and practicing compliance to engage fully in others. Meek people are unique and principled in every interaction.

Don't get caught up in thinking forceful and aggressive are more successful traits. Believing yielding in a compliant manner makes one weak is incorrect. Show people how meekness makes us different from others and strengthen our reputation as a someone who helps others succeed. Putting others needs above self-gain is right and noble. It sets us apart. Understanding how to use meekness as a real, tangible strength shows we are a connecting powerhouse. People that show their true weakness begin show others they put their own interests and need first. Don't ever feel meek equals weak. Weak people force themselves on others. Meek people lift others in interactions.

---

## CONNECTING CONCEPTS

- ➤ **Be humbly patient**--Keep meekness prominent in interactions.
- ➤ **Tempering thoughts of being dominant in the interaction**--Resisting urges to lead interactions is a strength of great connectors.
- ➤ **Docile is a strength when interacting with others**--Play to that strength.

---

## FORCE MEEKNESS? BAD IDEA.

I can only remember a few times Dad forced me to do anything. When I was 15, our church needed a Bass player to help our Music department. Typically, that meant playing a Bass guitar, which I later learned. At the time, my Legally-blind uncle played a Baby grand piano and a friend played drums. That was our Music department. We had a keyboard that split sounds, meaning the bottom or bass half replicated a Bass guitar sound while the upper end retained the piano sound. One day, Dad had an idea. To give our church the needed Bass sound, I would play just the bottom end of the keyboard like a Bass guitar. I objected at first but was overruled. Dad knew we had a need and I could fill it. End of discussion. The first Sunday was rough. I got markedly better until there was no discernable difference between playing a Bass guitar and what I was replicating. Dad knew what he was doing.

At times, we force ourselves to do something such as exercising, quitting smoking, drinking alcohol, avoiding eating sweets or consuming Carbonated beverages. Forcing ourselves to intentionally do something or not do something is one of the greatest challenges of life. It changes entire thought processes and ways of doing things forcing us to live without comfortable, old habits. Many times, new habits formed become better for us than old habits. Forcing ourselves into new habits for the sake of something different can yield disastrous results. It's contradictory to how habits form. A habit change needs a measure of success for sustainability. The discomfort of implementing new habits can push us to the brink of returning to the old habit. If we punish ourselves or using negative reinforcement, the old habit will return with a vengeance, primarily out of sheer rebellion. Changing behaviors with positive outcomes in mind fuels the catalyst for the change and stamps out rebellious temptations.

When forcing things to happen in rebellion, we make more mistakes. By forcing meekness, we mistakenly come across as not believable or connecting. It's akin to taking a shy person and making them the life of the party. It's an abject failure. Forcing meekness isn't genuine; people see right through it and run from it. Used genuinely, meekness is powerful and people are drawn to it like a magnet. Those harnessing the power of meekness and refuse to weaponize it for their ultimate glory become giants to others. The Bible says, "For everyone who exalts himself will be humbled, and he who habitually humbles himself will be exalted." It's the opposite of today's worldview that people should exalt themselves. We need more people who act the Scriptural way and are boldly meek. By habitually humbling ourselves, everyone will know who we are. Learning not to force meekness is a game-changer in our connecting abilities and . It will takes us a long way.

---

## CONNECTING CONCEPTS

➢ **Be comfortable being meek**--When we're comfortable, it's never forced.
➢ **Practice meekness**--It builds confidence and becomes naturally executed.
➢ **Be genuine**--Meekness should be a large part of our personality like a warm smile or kind words

---

## LEARN MEEKNESS FOR LIFE.

When I was six, my parents thought it would be good for me to learn the piano. As I mentioned earlier, I sang with Dad in our church at a three-year old and by this time, I sang well. Playing an instrument was logical. Mom picked me up from school and three days a week, took me to a local Record/Music shop. A sweet lady from our church worked there and gave Piano lessons. I was rambunctious, had the attention span of a dust mite and wouldn't sit still. My downfall was at-home practice. I hated it. In my young mind, practice wasn't nearly as important as watching Batman (the 1960's version). Four years later, as an Eleven-year-old, I took Piano lessons again, this time with a teacher that demanded practice. This piano teacher didn't care what was more important to me. Practice was mandatory or face an unhappy teacher who scolded me. Looking back, she was trying to instill something unnatural in me. Years later, I play piano pretty well by learning the value of practice.

Meekness isn't a skill or habit immediately picked up. It's not a natural personality tendency. Consistent meekness is intentional. It takes putting ourselves in situations to demonstrate meekness to others by using something uncomfortable in our makeup. My natural style is to be leading, prodding and moving the process forward in a compelling, dynamic manner. Yet, meekness causes me to deliver the same information and compelling facts in a way that puts it in the forefront and allows it to be the star. It's like starting to use the Non-dominant hand. With practice, the more comfortable and confident we get. It's as natural as using the Dominant hand. A great challenge is becoming great at skills not naturally dominant. Let's refer back to one of the definitions of meekness: Humbly patient or docile. It takes practice to be patient. It's an acquired skill. We're all, from the moment of birth, impatient. As babies, we cried to be fed, have a diaper changed or be held. As parents, children teach us patience. Like patience, meekness must be learned.

Many Business owners learn meekness quickly when sales and revenue don't come easily. Some become discouraged and walk away. Learning meekness makes us champions in business and life. Meekness waits for the right time to ask powerful questions and learns to understand people from their point of view, not ours. Meekness listens more than speaks and watches more than doing. Meekness working in us makes us not only complete people, but also superior, effortless value communicators. Meekness focuses on the necessary components to form unbreakable bonds. It teaches us to show up daily ready to connect.

Learning and demonstrating a life of meekness gives us completeness. Meekly humbling ourselves so people feel the ultimate sense of connection is incredible. Being docile so others feel empowered is liberating. Showing people intentional meekness is unmistakable. Learning meekness is one of the greatest lessons of life and. It's a gift that gives eternally.

---

## CONNECTING CONCEPTS

> **Deploy a calm demeanor in volatile situations--** This shows extreme humble patience.
> **Control the urge to be dominant--**Submit the conversation to the other person.
> **Invite others to select topics of conversation--**Let them choose something important to them.

---

## INHERIT MORE THAN THE EARTH.

Inheritances can be blessings or curses. I've never inherited a large sum of money, but know those who have. After my Weight-loss surgery in 2009, Dad invited me over to his house one Saturday to shop his closet. I was losing weight faster than my clothes could keep up. Even if I bought new clothes, they were quickly too big, as I wasn't yet at my Target weight. When I got to 220 pounds, Dad and I were roughly the same. I needed suits for church and Dad gave me six. Not only do I have suits, but I also wear a sweatshirt of his in the fall and winter every day after getting up because he wore it and will protect it with my life if necessary. I won't part with the things I have left of Dad's. It's my physical inheritance.

The greatest inheritance I received from Dad, though, were the traits, lessons and gifts he imparted. I know how to give, treat people well, the value of work, what to say and how to say it because of Dad. Those traits inherited from him will live on as I pass those things to my son. The inheritance I treasure most from Dad were the times, laughs and talks we shared. Those moments and memories shaped me into the man I am today and are the things that truly last. That's an eternal inheritance.

What would life be like inheriting millions of dollars? Suddenly, with a dying breath, we're instantly wealthy. Life would be much different. We could travel the world and do anything we desired. To work or not work, is entirely up to us. By the simple fact of being born into a certain family, we hit the lottery. Inheritance doesn't account for the hard work, blood, sweat and tears of the person leaving the inheritance. The person receiving rarely tastes any of that. They simply reap the reward. With the stroke of a pen, they inherit something that took years to acquire and accumulate. Two things happen to inheritances. They're either squandered away or passed on to future generations continuing its impact. Inheritances are so powerful by being awe-inspiring or feeling like carrying the weight of the world.

When meekness is at work in our lives, we inherit far more than material things. We inherit deeper, stronger relationships, more satisfaction and a greater understanding of life. Meekness personified allows others to see us in the light we're destined to walk. I have inherited customers, territories and relationships formed by others. There were days I felt totally inadequate. I had to humble myself. I wasn't the one who built the relationship. I had to practice meekness. We can inherit valuable behaviors but shouldn't be copycats. People see right through it. We interject our inherited abilities and gifts into every relationship and become earth-shattering connectors.

Inheriting meekness is daunting. We can feel as though heavy armor has been put on us and we must deftly function in it. Deft meekness ensures different connection. Meekness may not look like much on the surface, but inheriting it is a priceless treasure. By demonstrating meekness, we give untold riches in each interaction. A person rich in meekness shares the wealth in spades with others. They understand the shoulders of others that helped lift them to success. We don't climb there by ourselves. Meekness shows us how appreciate others every day. People never see how a situation affects us positively or negatively due to inheriting great internal strength through meekness. We can lose a great relationship or have a great personal or professional triumph. By inheriting meekness, most will never know it.

Meekness is the gift of a lifetime. Why did Jesus say that the meek would inherit the earth? Their attitude and spirit endear them to so many that men will truly give into their bosom. People see a difference when those clothed in meekness walk into a room. Walk a day in meekness, be intentional with it and show others a priceless inheritance. Meekness shows others transformative power that radiates everywhere in everyone. Meekness magnified is strength personified.

## CONNECTING CONCEPTS

➤ **Be free with giving meekness**--Give it to everyone in every interaction.

➤ **Meekness is not patented**--By sharing meekness, show its ability to transform situations.

➤ **Teach meekness**--Demonstrate to others how to have the same level of meekness in their own lives.

Me, Dad and my son, Bryce singing together at Dad's
church in Chesapeake, Ohio, Father's Day 2011.

# CHAPTER 5

## *People Buy Observant*

D ad gave me a physical trait I've since passed to my son... Flat feet. In late 1972, as a 19-year-old new father, Dad's Draft number was called, as the Vietnam War was in full force. Then, the United States didn't have a Professional military. If a person didn't voluntarily enlist, they could be chosen in the Selective Service Draft. During the war, Draft Lottery Television shows revealed numbers selected for immediate enlistment and deployment. Depending on someone's birthday, males ranging from 18 to 22 received a Draft number after registering as mandated by Federal law. One night while watching television, Dad's Draft number was displayed. He was distraught. He didn't want to leave me and Mom and go to the other side of the world. Few drafted young men wanted to go to Vietnam due to fear of not coming home alive. As Dad made his way to the Draft station for his physical, he connected with the doctor conducting the Head-to-Toe examination. Doctors wouldn't pass anyone with any kind of physical defect, especially the flat-footed. They weren't able to run well in Vietnamese jungles. Noticing my Dad's Flat feet, the doctor failed Dad's physical. By failing the physical, a person couldn't be drafted again. A quick observation of something obscure saved Dad's life.

Many years later when my son was a boy, my wife had him at our local Mall playing in the Play area which require those inside it to remove their shoes. As my son was playing, a man walked up to my wife and said to her, "Is that your son? I couldn't help noticing his feet." He explained that he was with the Shriners organization. They provided foot care free of charge for children with Flat feet and gave her his card. Relieved, my wife thanked him. Having seen knee issues with my own flat feet, she saw the opportunity to get our son corrective insoles that helped him as he grew. That man helped our son by being observant. Those insoles helped avoid issues as he grew. That man, who we haven't seen since, understood the importance of observing.

Yogi Berra, Hall of Fame Baseball catcher said, "You can observe a lot by watching." That's a powerful statement in connecting. We focus on saying the right things in every interaction. Verbal communication is emphasized. Voice inflection, diction, correct phrasing and wording are stressed. Communicating correctly are taught and trained as foundational principles of relationship building. Just as important is the skill of observation. Many aren't as observant to connect at the deepest level with people.

What is observant? Dictionary.com defines observant as: "Quick to notice or perceive; alert. Looking at, watching or regarding attentively; watchful." Merriam-Webster adds: "Keen, perceptive; paying strict attention; mindful." It's listening with our eyes. We spend more time training on and practicing listening and little time on observation. We gain critical information about people by observing them. Many times, I've connected powerfully by pointing out something observed incredibly important to the other person. In my 24-year marriage, I've gotten a kiss and a smile from my wife by observing something she'd done to her hair, a dress she wore, her nails or a scarf and pointed it out. Observation is impactful.

Let's opine for a bit on observation.

## WATCH JUST A MOMENT.

The first time I played golf with Dad, I was a teenager. I watched him tee off and couldn't believe how far he hit the ball. Years later, when I played with Dad, my cousins and uncle, they all hit the ball a mile. I stood and stared at every drive. When I finally connected on a big drive, I stared at it. I was in awe that I hit a ball equally as far. Golfers booming a drive off the tee or a baseball player hitting a mammoth Home run admire what they accomplished. Staring too long looks arrogant in that moment.

Try the staring at something for one minute. The eyes begin drifting the closer the minute comes. When staring at our spouse for a minute, we cause discomfort in them. Stare at a stranger for 30 seconds and it will get tense quickly. Most people aren't comfortable with long stares. Looking at things too long isn't normal. Our attention spans can't handle that type of focus and isn't in our best interest to stare at things too long.

Make quick glances on items or things that catch our attention. Things caught and stored in the memory can be recalled at key points in conversations or as conversation starters. When conducting In-Home interviews of Prospective students while working in the Higher Education space, I used objects in their surroundings to build rapport. A picture on the fireplace, a shirt the student wore or a Class ring on the hand were great ways to be personally observant. Capturing the intimate surroundings of others pays the greatest non-verbal gesture of respect.

Quick observational looks at objects or items offer a brief look inside a person's personality. Those items in their surroundings evokes emotion and encourages deeper conversation to build connection. People connect more readily and much faster with people that notice personal things. Ladies appreciate tasteful, sincere complements about articles of clothing. Men appreciate compliment on a shirt, tie or shoes. Compliments come from good observation. People like knowing other people notice. Lots of conversations move forward by simply talking about what's observed.

Great observers don't need to pick out five or six things in a room to start a conversation. They need one. Find one thing that catches attention to bring to the other person's attention. Getting into a staring contest with one item in the other person's surroundings puts undue pressure on us to force that item into conversation. Don't fall into that trap. Glance, file and recall.

Focusing on connecting and building rapport. Think simply, think quickly. Let the other person fill in the details of the item, not the other way around. The other person will detail the significance of the item. Just bring it up. Here's an example. "John, I noticed your picture with the President of the United States. Tell me about that experience." If it was memorable, we open an amazing door of connection, simply by paying attention. People observe those that observe important things to them. Everyone has things of value. Find those things and use them to unlock a multitude of opportunities.

---

## CONNECTING CONCEPTS

➢ **Some things catch our eyes right away**--Use that technique when starting relationships.

➢ **Glance at things previously unnoticed**--Take the observation skill to the Next level.

➢ **Conversation starters are everywhere**--From previous recall, know where to look next.

---

## PRIORITIZE OTHER PEOPLE'S PROPERTY.

In our Living room, we have pictures of Dad, my wife's late father and my wife's Grandparents together, taken right after our wedding in 1996. We have a rocking chair that belonged to my late Grandmother Sexton we inherited after Dad passed away. In my Podcast studio at home, I record *The Intentional Encourager Podcast* in Dad's Desk chair he sat in to study for sermons, do work and pay bills. A picture of Dad taken in Alaska that was displayed at his Memorial service hangs over my work desk. We have things around our house valuable to us from people no longer with us. Everyone has things they're proud to display. When I need a professional background for video conversations, I have my Masters of Business Administration degree, Personalized Autographed pictures, baseballs from games my son played in High School, my High school baseball hat, that rest on a bookcase that hold signed books from dear friends who wrote them. I treasure these things and why I hold on to them. Each item has its own unique meaning.

Those items aren't for me to brag or boast. I love Autographed items, especially from people I admire. My son has a framed Lebron James Autographed jersey prominently displayed in his room. He has something his favorite Basketball player and one of the greatest to play the game has personally signed. He's proud of it, as well he should be. He also has an old bookshelf in his room belonging to his maternal grandfather that he keeps eclectic things. When he was a kid, he collected Snow globes and still displays those on that bookshelf alongside a Wheaties box that has a picture we took when he was a baby. Those things are treasures because they invoke strong memories. We all have specific things that mean something to us as well and other possessions that mean everything to us.

When we're in the intimate setting of others, they often display personal items of great pride. Those items revealing details about who they are and experiences that shape them. Insignificant items likely wouldn't be displayed. I have a longtime friend who runs a nearly 125-store Pizza chain. In his office, mounted on the wall above his desk is a Marlin caught many years ago on a fishing trip and across the room, pictures of him with various Professional golfers and other unique items of significance. These are glimpses into his life and experiences he's proud to share. Many people are proud of the things in their office or work surroundings. Maybe there's a framed picture on the wall of them with someone famous that might also be personally autographed. There may be books on the desk of professional or personal impact.

Items are small windows into one's personality. Personalities connect with like personalities. Tap into others' personalities by the things they display. Something may evoke an emotion in them like Dad's chair does for me in my Home office. Great connectors understand where and when to use those things to connect to the significance and importance of others. Typically, we aren't likely to see a framed Speeding ticket for going 120 in a 55 and getting charged with Reckless driving or "lucky" Boxer shorts hanging on someone's wall. They hold no meaning.

People display things with meaning. Go to that place with that person and connect to it. I can look at things in my house that mean something and feel the emotional attachment. Ask me about an item and I'll instantly connect. I'm not hanging a picture up in my office of someone I've never met or had any personal connection. I do, however, have a picture of the Southern Gospel quartet I helped establish 12 years ago hanging in my office. Those men are my brothers. I want people to see that picture. Those same things we see in intimate settings mean something to the other person.

Meet people in those moments through those items. Talk about those things, and gain deeper insight into the life, personality and the heart of others. People love talking about things that mean something to them. Those are interactions worth having and observations worth making. We not only will see unusual, incredible things, and but get obvious glimpses into the lives of people.

---

## CONNECTING CONCEPTS

➤ **Ask the other person for permission to discuss an item--** "I noticed that picture. Would you mind telling me more about it?"

➤ **Craft a follow-up question to take a deeper interest**--It propels conversation forward. "That must have been an exciting trip. What made you decide to go there?"

➤ **Ask what that item truly means to that person--** "What immediately comes to mind when you see this?"

---

## THINK OBVIOUS, NOT OBLIVIOUS.

Dad wasn't one to say things twice. Growing up, if he told my sister and I to do something, we did it the first time. If Dad spoke again, there was trouble. We never said, "I didn't hear you." "I didn't see that." "What do you want?" Dad was clear. If he wanted something done, it was to be executed then and there. No questions asked. It was obvious what he meant. Dad never hinted; he'd say it. If we walked around oblivious, it was obvious we were going to feel his wrath. Dad taught us to look at everything around us. He wasn't going to tell us to pick up something left on the couch. If it was in his spot, he moved it. If it stayed there, it wasn't good. We learned not to leave things lying around. I must admit in my own home today, I do leave things at times. My wife is obvious to remind me and as with Dad, for peace in my home, I'd better not be oblivious. The same goes for my son with his mother.

The travel website, Travelocity, has a commercial featuring a character many have nicknamed a friend, family member or co-worker. "Captain Obvious" points out something or someone in wonderment that many around him have already realized. I've heard the phrase used as a derogatory term when someone makes a statement that appears to be a no-brainer. In connection, observing the obvious builds greater bonds between people. We do ourselves more connecting harm oblivious to something for fear of emphasizing the obvious. Obviously, in observing a person's surroundings and building stronger connections, we must see what they see. The old adage, "Beauty is in the eye of the beholder" must be applied.

In each interaction, behold things differently. Dad and I had different tastes, especially. There were times I'd wear something to church and he'd say, "Why are you wearing THAT?" Although, I'm 50% Dad, we saw fashion differently. Dad wanted to match. I wanted to match and stand out. Our connections are like that. They have traits they want to stand out. To connect stronger, we can't be oblivious. We need to match. In the same way we avoid mismatching clothing, obviously, avoid mismatching in interactions.

At times, we may be oblivious where to match with others. For instance, some people have an obvious physical defect, birthmark,

PEOPLE BUY FROM PEOPLE

scar or other impediment. We're fearful that inquiring about it might cause hurt feelings. It's obvious they get asked about it and we don't know how to approach it, especially in building the relationship. Don't ignore it. Some find being oblivious to their defect is hurtful and disrespectful. They may have a powerful story behind it. Graciously ask permission to hear it to know that person deeper. Defects also occur in our relationships. We become oblivious to issues when things appear to be good. It's small. No big deal.

When it rains, we see it. That's obvious. Water coming into the house from too much rain isn't the time to be oblivious. On a June day in 2016, most of West Virginia got a rainstorm forecasted the night before by Meteorologists around the state. When it began, people went about the day oblivious to it. Quickly and obviously, parts of West Virginia got nearly 12 inches of rain and experienced historic, catastrophic flooding. The devastation nearly 100 miles wide. No one was prepared for the damage incurred. We're oblivious to devastating damage to relationships until massive cleanup is obvious.

Problems expose the fact that we became oblivious. When someone puts on 50 pounds, they were oblivious to the obvious. Eat more than we move and we gain weight. Begin dismissing things in relationships and our oblivion is obvious. When my wife does something different in her appearance, she'll ask, "Do you like it?" I have to be obvious and notice. We can't point out the obvious with others and be oblivious to their reaction. Relationships need obvious positive reinforcement and not oblivious selfishness. When people hurt, they seek help. In the Bible, a traveler was mugged, beaten and left for dead. People passed and offered no help. The Good Samaritan didn't. He wasn't oblivious. He was obvious in helping the wounded traveler recover. Are we oblivious to the needs of others or are we obvious connectors, keeping others first? It's obvious how great connectors answer that question. Avoiding the oblivious ensures a full picture of every detail allowing us not to miss the small things.

<br>

---

## CONNECTING CONCEPTS

➤ **When there's more to understand, uncover it--**
Delve deeper without interrogation.
➤ **Don't be oblivious to the details of one's story--**It
better explains the plot.
➤ **Stay current--**Periodic observations in relationships
expose previously missed variances.

---

## FOCUS ON KNICK-KNACKS AND PRETTIES.

Growing up, Mom had knick-knacks all around our house. She
called them "pretties." Most of them were glass figurines she considered pretty. Being all boy and loving anything with a ball or
made into a ball, I played ball in the house. On several occasions,
Dad played with me and if we broke one of the pretties, it wasn't
pleasant from Mom. Gluing a broken part back on didn't remedy
the problem. Mom cooled off after a while and Dad and I learned
to put the pretties where they wouldn't get broken. My wife collects
pretties called Willow Tree figurines. Those figurines are handled
with care when I dust our house. If one breaks, it's not a good day
for me. Fortunately, my son was a Video game kid, so he didn't
replicate what I did for indoor entertainment.

Knick-knacks and pretties are found in many homes and offices.
Things, trinkets, snow-globes or awards that have meaning. In "The
Office," many remember Michael Scott's "Dundie Awards." The
Dundies were a unique way to recognize employees for various
things around the office. I have knick-knacks in my office I enjoy
looking at from time to time. Yes, I've even broken a few of my
own pretties. (I'm just as disgusted as Mom was when it happens.)
Those knick-knacks give a glimpse into my personality.

Knick-knacks are personal pieces of people and serve as reminders of powerful relationships, experiences or emotions. A seashell

recalls the vacation of a lifetime. A trinket made by their child invokes sentimental memories. A golf ball relives a special day on the course. A bronzed baby shoe, a permanent reminder of the power of being a parent. These aren't insignificant things to others, rather, hold wonderful clues unlocking who they truly are. Knick-knacks don't just take up space on a desk or shelf, they contain unforgettable stories.

Don't discount knick-knacks, invite their story. As the story is told, notice facial expressions and hear the vocal emotion with genuine intent. Take in every word. Pointing out the smallest things shows others how different we are. Everyone looks at pictures on the wall or the occasional trophy mount. We'll talk in just a moment about trophies, plaques and awards. Sincere interest in a knick-knack catches attention and captures connection. Don't focus solely on the big things in the room or on the desk. Focus on the small, important things right in front of us.

As more interactions happen virtually, look at things immediately around the other person. This is a great Scavenger hunt of things to use to connect and deepen relationships. I use Zoom to record audio and video episodes of *The Intentional Encourager Podcast.* Before recording, I'll see what's in the other person's surroundings that triggers a question asked in the podcast. Many times, it's a small item that leads to a great question. People care when asked about something they see every day. Intentionally ask, engage and connect around those seemingly insignificant items. My friend, Damon Burton, Author of Outrank, sends personalized trinkets to his friends. Those items occupying spots on desks, walls and bookshelves and better yet, places in their hearts.

Shared experiences can be so powerful, people keep a memento of it and cherish it. Each time look at it, they're reminded them of the deep bond we've built with them and their importance to us. THAT'S the pretty power of a knick-knack.Most of the time, Ppeople often keep the most valuable pretties in a case.

## CONNECTING CONCEPTS

➤ **Start small**--The smallest things often have the greatest impact.
➤ **Check the hands**--A class ring or other ring leads to incredible conversations.
➤ **Compliment what's seen**--People love sincere compliments.

## REVERE THE TROPHY CASE.

In my Pastor's office is a glass bookcase containing Bibles from his late Great-Grandparents, Grandparents and mother, who were Pastors and Missionaries. Each Bible is precious and valuable to him serving as a reminder of his Family heritage. Looking at the Bibles, the pages are worn and the covers tattered. The bookcase provides protection and an opportunity to tell stories of those who possessed them. I'm sure he's tempted to go over to the case, open it and hold a Bible in his hands, reading from the pages his ancestors read before him. There are hand-written notes in the margins from things gleaned from the Word of God that provides insight to thoughts when the notation was penned.

To someone looking inside the case, they might find it interesting or fascinating to see the Bibles. To my Pastor, these are trophies of Heroes of the Faith reminding him of his lineage in ministry, keeping him grounded, showing a glimpse into Pastoring and the ultimate joys of ministry. They are personal, relational and emotional. Old Bibles that would bring a few dollars to a collector are priceless to my Pastor who cherishes them.

The Trophy case is where "the good stuff" is kept and the spot where professional and personal accomplishments with awards attached to them are kept for posterity. Walk into most High schools and the Trophy case is prominent. Visitors can visually see the historical accomplishments of that school. Displayed in these cases are Athletic trophies, plaques, awards, letters, jerseys, basketballs, footballs, baseballs and basketball nets from significant moments or people in the school's history commemorated, celebrated and memorialized. The trophy case is an inspiration and reminder to students and alumni of the fabric of that school's existence.

Great achievers love accomplishments. Some professionals have awards displayed that serve as daily reminders to where they came from, where they've been and where they're going. I remember the first significant Sales award I received in 2001. As a Territory Manager for a Foodservice distributor, I had a phenomenal Sales year won Sales Person of the Year, the highest Sales award in our company. It came with a big check and big trophy. Because of its size, we decided to get rid of the trophy, but kept the nameplate on it listing the accomplishment, the year and my name. I've forgotten the trophy, but will never forget the accomplishment.

People love to display their accomplishments. Just as knick-knacks, pictures and mementos spark emotions about people and experiences, trophies, plaques and awards evoke emotions about accomplishment. An award's significance reminds them of the sacrifice, blood, sweat and tears that went into earning it. They'll tell the story of what it took when asked. There could be wisdom passed, encouragement to glean and connection strengthened. Take them back to that time and watch them swell with pride. When noticing and recognizing awards, we validate people and their prowess. Some are humbled by this acknowledgement while others expect it.

Avoid bringing personal correlation to an award unless it adds greater value to the other person. Our sole goal is to create, build, foster and cement relationships. We focus the discussion on their accomplishments, not ours. Those symbols of accomplishment are visible reminders of success and signify the person who received them is worthy of merit by their work, actions and diligence. With genuine interest and respect, award others the highest honor by honoring them. Lessons shared from those conversations make us better. They may have overcome a challenge we struggle to conquer.

Take notes, if possible. When recognizing others' achievements, we unlock emotion and remind them of the journey. Unlocking emotions with a smile, a sigh, wistful glance or a look of consternation builds bonds with others. Settle in and connect.

When recognizing and valuing achievements and desiring to know more about them, we go to a different place with others. Behavior like that is uncommon and award-winning. When we observe what others don't, we see what others can't.

---

## CONNECTING CONCEPTS

➤ **Ask for an explanation**—Don't assume meaning. Get their explanation of the award's meaning.

➤ **Let a modest person be modest**--Gracefully move the conversation forward if others are uncomfortable with attention.

➤ **Don't compare trophies**--Build up others' awards even if we have a truckload of them ourselves.

---

Mom and Dad in Alaska, Summer 2011, a 40th Wedding Anniversary gift from their church.

# CHAPTER 6

# *People Buy Engaging*

From the minute Dad entered a room, he was engaging. Dad shined at funerals. I watched him engage with people he hadn't seen in years as if he'd seen them the day before. Dad believed engagement showed deep care for others. As a Pastor, his church had dinners after service every other Sunday. Dad believed meals were perfect opportunities to engage. As a family, Dad made sure we came together most every Saturday for a meal to engage with his kids and especially, his grandkids. Engagement was the chance to connect with us collectively and individually. When we were at his house, sometimes it would be just he and I sitting and watch a sporting event on television, talking and sharing. I loved those times and would give anything now for five minutes of engagement with Dad.

What comes to mind when we hear the word "engaging?" Warm? Inviting? Captivating? Engaging is an adjective that means "charming and attractive." Let's move deeper into the synonyms of engaging. Great connectors are known by these words. "Appealing; delightful; agreeable; pleasant; likeable; pleasing; captivating" Who doesn't want to be appealing, likeable and captivating? We all do. Zig Ziglar said, "People love to buy. They hate to be sold." People

crave engagement over transaction and be captivated, not manip-
ulated. It's about the experience more than purchase.

Today, engagement with companies begins with a few mouse
clicks on a laptop or on our phones through an App. Diligent
customers choose the level of engagement as companies attempt
to influence on Social media, television and radio advertisements
with enough education to comfortably make a buying decision.
They want to understand buying motives and send targeted messaging around those motives. It's logical on the surface. However,
customer feel attacked instead of engaged. People should never
feel that our engagement attacks them and will retreat in those
instances. Why would anyone connect like that? Most don't know
better and aren't equipped to engage people correctly.

Correct engagement is strategically effective and significant
in growing our network, personally and professionally. Let's discuss Social media briefly. There's a myriad of platforms where
people engage. Yet, we find more self-centered, instigating,
propaganda-promoting and sometimes vile posts than actual
engaging discussion where value is transferred. I care for people
posting a life-altering event or something of value to share. I don't
care about vacation pictures or Current events memes. Many don't
realize they have a valuable engagement tool in their hands and
few uses it intelligently.

People desire deeper engagement, not more minutia. For gifted
connectors, daily engagement is an art form offering the correct
balance of information, entertainment, joy, comfort and trust. They
invite connections into virtual conversation and compel them to
stay. They make others feel involved and look forward to the next
interaction. THAT'S engagement! Great engagement is unique.
Great connectors find ways to give others that feeling every time.
Nothing beats great engagement!

Let's expound upon exquisite engagement.

## GLEAN FROM THE STARTER AND FLYWHEEL.

On a Friday afternoon in December 2011 while sitting in my house, my cell phone rang. It was Dad. I figured he was calling about my seeing my family the next day. Instead, it was a call for help. Dad didn't call for help. I usually called him for it. He explained, "Son, you know I'm pastoring and working a six-state territory. I met with my boss, told him I needed help and he agreed. I need you." I was stunned. At that time, I worked evenings and my schedule was misaligned with my family's schedule. We were together on the weekend. I wanted to help Dad, but how would this affect our relationship? I just wanted him to be Dad, but he wanted us working together. After getting past some initial objections, we pursued the opportunity.

In February 2012, Dad picked me up for our first day of work together and hit the road. We had places to go, and I had people to meet. I saw a spark in Dad's eye and he was eager to introduce me to his professional world. It had a "Dynamic Duo" feel and we were ready to serve notice on our competitors. It remains the best job of my life and nothing comes close. When I joined the company, I introduced Marketing and Sales ideas and brought focus and customer engagement to other Profit-makers in our product offering. For the first few weeks, though, my head was spinning. I knew Sales, Marketing and Territory Management but knew NOTHING about Starters, Alternators and the component parts to rebuild them. Dad explained products and functions in ways I understood. I was, and still am, mechanically incompetent.

The first mechanical thing I learned about a starter is its only function is turning over a motor through engagement. On the front of the starter is a round component with teeth, called the drive, that engages with the flywheel when powered by the battery and meshes. In an "Old school" application, the drive rammed violently into the flywheel to engage meshing. For generations, this was the only technology that existed. Today, a Soft-Start engagement is the standard where the starter drive meshes into a proper fit with the flywheel, allows the starter and flywheel to last longer.

How do we mesh correctly with people for longer-lasting relationships? By being "Soft-starters." Some believe they should engage by banging into people and forcing the connection. There's no meshing. Saturating people into engagement is disastrous strategy. It borders on poor manners and simple human decency. People are more engagement aware now more than ever. Engagement without meshing is not only hard to do but even harder to sustain. We should never pressure people to engage. The way we engage should speak for itself. People want to be welcomed to engage and engage softly and comfortably in interactions. Soft engagement is a beautiful thing to watch and an even better to facilitate.

The enjoyment of meshing is building relationships in a repeatable, consistent process. Soft engagers understand all different types of personality styles and the dynamics of Relationship building. Watch the room at a Networking event. Some people are natural engagers. A particular interaction I remember well was with a Senior company executive. We were enjoying a conversation when a colleague interrupted and asked for a moment of her time. I excused myself and went to find a beverage. Nearly 10 minutes later, the executive found me and said, "Let's pick up our conversation." This is natural engagement. Though layers apart organizationally, we weren't layers apart relationally.

Great connectors understand the importance of meshing and adapt their personalities with other styles. They use consistent messaging, eye contact and sincere facial expressions to build connective bridges. They don't have to force meshing. People are eager and ready to receive their message. For them, meshing is not a pugilistic activity and there's never an internal fight for their message to connect. Their soft, smooth engagement every time makes meshing easy. Component need other components to mesh. They never engage solo.

## CONNECTING CONCEPTS

➤ **Know the other person's personality type.** Mesh with their tone and pace.

➤ **Know a couple of things that turns over the internal motor of others.** Mesh with what interests them.

➤ **Get a feel for how people engage.** Some seek engagement while others are more comfortable being engaged.

## FLY THE PLANE SOLO?

I get my love of comedies from Dad. If a movie on television made him laugh, we watched it. I remember watching the 1980 classic slapstick comedy *Airplane!* with Dad. There's a scene onboard an aircraft full of passengers where the pilot, played by Robert Slack and the Co-pilot, played by Kareem Abdul-Jabbar, are both incapacitated and the plane is plummeting to disaster. One of the passengers, Ted Striker, played by Robert Hays, was a former fighter pilot traumatized in war and developed a fear of flying. However, when his girlfriend, a flight attendant, leaves him, he gets on the plane determined to win her back. As the events unfold, the passengers learn Striker is a former pilot and beg him to intervene. Striker takes control of the plane with the assistance of his mentor and a veteran pilot, Rex Kramer, played by Lloyd Bridges. Striker overcomes his fears, lands the plane, saves the passengers and gets his girl, all while hilarity and chaos ensue.

According to Wikipedia, the requirement for a first "Solo" flight as a pilot is to have 10 to 30 hours of flight time. Things a pilot should be able to do before soloing is knowing how to successfully maneuver takeoffs, landings and traffic patterns. Pilots learn under the careful guidance of an experienced instructor that observes successful executions and guides through potentially troubling situations. No Commercial aircraft flies on Auto pilot or with a single pilot at the controls. The Co-Pilot is critically important. The Co-Pilot not only helps navigate a flight in concert with the Pilot, but takes control in case of emergency. Likely, a short flight could be done solo, but why risk passenger safety? Great communication is necessary between Pilot and Co-Pilot to keep the flight on course.

When connecting with people, great communication keeps interactions on course to the desired destination. The Pilot can't decide to take the plane in one direction and the Co-Pilot decides to take it another. We shouldn't steer interactions off course. The interaction will crash. It's called Catastrophic failure. In situations of a mechanical failure, the Pilot and Co-Pilot work together to plan for the safest landing possible, even if it's an emergency landing to protect all passengers. There are times when the mechanics of an interaction break down. We have to keep the interaction airborne at all costs. Work together with others to make every interaction and smooth and comfortable ride.

In certain situations, we may be tempted to fly solo and navigate the interaction. We've got the necessary experience to take people to our destination. The direction is clear, the course set. Just sit back, relax and enjoy the flight. This is dangerous. Without engagement, we're more likely to crash and burn. That's a horrific feeling. A member of my wife's family was killed in a Single-engine plane crash along with her father, who was the pilot, and her boyfriend. This was devastating and life-changing to the family. The experienced pilot had flown his plane hundreds of times and come back safely each time. This flight turned dangerous quickly because he couldn't maneuver his way out of disaster. That tragedy has a literal and figurative reminder about the dangers of flying solo and the lives impacted by it.

I'm not flippantly comparing connecting to a tragic event like a plane crash where lives are lost, rather, drawing a parallel. Safety first is not simply a cool motto, but a life-saving credo. Pilots don't take unnecessary risks. It's just not worth it. It's why they don't fly in blizzards or severe thunderstorms. In the same respect, we jeopardize valuable relationships not safely interacting with the others. People need to be a part of the connecting process, not watching it fly solo. The last thing we need is someone halt an interaction's takeoff and grounding the process. The most frustrating thing in the world is to be at the airport waiting for a flight only to have it canceled. When we fly solo around people in connecting, interactions get cancelled. We don't want that reputation. The best part of a flight is seeing the plane get nearer and nearer to the ground. That's a safe connection.

---

## CONNECTING CONCEPTS

- ➤ **The most skilled connectors need connecting co-pilots**—They can't connect without them.
- ➤ **If people aren't instruments of connection, relationship crash**—Be an instrument reader.
- ➤ **The safest direction we steer relationships is toward the same place**—Interactions avoid turbulence when everyone looks for smooth air.

---

## DRAW PEOPLE NEARER.

Musically, Dad raised me on Gospel hymns. When visiting another church, before a service, I read hymnals. At churches we attended, Dad lead the Congregational singing from hymnals. We sang songs such as, "All in Him"; "Blessed Assurance"; "Fill My Way Every Day with Love" and "Oh, How I Love Jesus." I hear Dad sing those songs in my mind as though he's singing next to me. Those were precious and wonderful times. Dad sang those songs because he loved the lyric and wouldn't sing a song that didn't contain soul-stirring lyrics. The power of words moved Dad.

One hymn I recall singing as a kid was "Draw Me Nearer." As it did with Dad, its words have often ministered to me. The songwriter was a lady named Frances J. "Fanny" Crosby. According to Wikipedia, Crosby was born in March of 1820 and died in February 1915 at 94. Blind from birth, she wrote nearly 8,000 songs including: Pass Me Not O' Gentle Savior, I Am Thine O' Lord, He Hideth My Soul, Near the Cross and Blessed Assurance. In 1843, she was the first woman to speak before the United States Senate arguing for support for education for the blind. In 1859, Fanny had a daughter that died not long after her birth, of what many believe to be SIDS (Sudden Infant Death Syndrome). This would be the only child she would bear. Her tune, "Safe in The Arms of Jesus" was inspired by the infant's death. Fanny lived a hard life, taken advantage of by publishers who paid her little royalties for her songs, separated from her husband and involved in disputes with family and close friends. Her songs through rich tones of poetry and lyrical integrity were no doubt drawn from incredible struggles. "Draw Me Nearer" is no different. Crosby likely wrote this song from a deep desire to be as close to God as humanly possible and for Him to draw her nearer daily. Do we have a strong desire to draw close to others?

We cherish close relationships with those we care for and love. Every interaction must seek to draw near to fulfilling relationships in business, ministry and life. However, we can choose another path by pushing people away through ambivalence. We either like someone or we don't. There's no middle ground. There are people we just don't like. Maybe they aren't kind people or we don't see eye to eye. We don't get that warm, fuzzy feeling in interactions. We might sit in the car for 10 minutes dreading our impending time with them. For me, that was the case visiting my Mom's Father (Papaw) and Step-mother (Mamaw).

Papaw was much different than me. I liked sports, he liked to fish. He and Dad were different as night and day. When my sister and I were kids, we did a lot with my Grandparents, but that changed when they adopted our uncle. The addition didn't draw us nearer, rather created a separating gulf. I loved them, but was never as close. One of the last conversations I remember with Papaw rebuilt a bridge. It was Thanksgiving 1991. As mentioned earlier, I worked in the Sports department of our local newspaper while in college. Each Monday, members of our local community wrote guest Opinion columns, called "The Armchair Quarterback" on a topic in the world of sports. I wrote my first "Armchair," a recap of the terrible 1991 Cincinnati Reds season, complete with a comprehensive breakdown of what the Reds needed to improve in 1992. As a daily subscriber to the newspaper, Papaw read it each morning with his coffee.

Sitting at the table before Thanksgiving dinner, he looked at me with his dark brown eyes and said, "I read your article in the paper. You did a fine job. I really enjoyed it." We hadn't bonded like that in a long time. I loved it. He drew me nearer with words of admiration. He was proud of me and I was so happy making Papaw proud. I felt close to him in that moment. A few months later, I sang at his funeral. The Thanksgiving conversation drew him nearer in my mind as I began singing to family and friends. One more time to be close to Papaw.

How do we powerfully pull people closer? Some might say, "We don't." That thinking keeps people from drawing people nearer. We must be intentional in drawing people closer. It's far more than pushing emotional hot buttons to evoke reaction or manufacturing feelings in an attempt to simply be connected. Be open to being open. We'll never draw people nearer by closing off personal things. People aren't robots. They have real feelings and emotions. In my life and career, I've drawn people closer by being an Amateur psychologist, listening to people share difficult personal and professional situations troubling them and praying with hurting people.

Nothing draws us nearer to people more than by showing love and compassion in times of crippling loss. The greatest way to draw people nearer is being genuine, kind and caring in good times and bad. Tragedy isn't the only thing that draws people closer. Go to weddings, ball games and other events. Do life with people and allow them space and room to share themselves. Draw them nearer by getting close to their heart and talking about things most precious to them. In turn, they are more interested in and what's close to our heart. It's awfully hard to pull someone away that draws themselves nearer.

Be intentional about the foundation of a person. People talk most about what and who they care about deepest. On the Home screen of my Cell phone there's a picture of my family and I on our June 2019 cruise. Asking about my family, my faith or my favorite sports teams draws me nearer. Care about and show genuine interest in what others care about, and we draw people powerfully nearer. Zap those small things in relationships that keeps people from drawing nearer.

---

## CONNECTING CONCEPTS

- ➢ **Consider how comfortable people are with getting closer**--Some have difficulty getting close to others.
- ➢ **Remove all pre-conceived notions as to ulterior motives**--Be noble in moving relationships closer.
- ➢ **See clearly how a close, deep relationship looks to both people**--Relationships can't be one-sided.

---

## ZAP PESTS AND PROBLEMS.

Twice in my childhood, my family and I lived in a Mobile Home park. Dad and Mom were always diligent about us having a good place to live, although, we didn't own our own home for a nearly 10-year stretch. In Mobile Home parks (also known as Trailer parks), many of our neighbors had bug zappers. Bug zappers are common in Appalachia, especially among the Trailer park community. In many places in our region, with a beverage nearby and sitting on a porch, watching a bug zapper in action is high-quality entertainment. Hillbillies and Rednecks of the last 35 years or so testify of the mesmerizing, hypnotic power of the Bug zapper. For those unaware of what a Bug zapper does, I'll explain. A Bug zapper hangs in high-traffic areas for mosquitos, like a porch.

The Bug zapper is round with a mesh covering around strings of blue, neon-like lights wrapping around the inside. The blue lights are designed to draw mosquitos to the zapper. The mesh covering allows the pests inside but not to come back out. To a mosquito, the lights look like a disco, enticing them to a mysterious, wonderful place, only to zap them into oblivion. When bugs are zapped, an electric-current type noise occurs, and the mosquito meets its doom. In an eye blink, mosquitos are wiped out by the Bug zapper. Gone are the days of swatting them away with a fly swatter, trying to smack one off your arm or the alluring scent of bug repellant. Keeping score of pests meeting their demise in a 15, 30, 45 or one-hour stretch, kicks the Entertainment value up a notch. It can be a glorious evening.

We all possess traits that attract people. The attraction of the mosquito to the bug zapper is light and sound, instinctively causing them to fearlessly fly to it. Do people see differences in us attracting them to what we offer and instinctively causing them to fearlessly move toward us? Our willingness to plug into people causes attraction. The great thing about a bug zapper is that it works in any outdoor space with access to a 110-volt power source. People want the power to eliminate problems overtaking them like a swarm of mosquitos that bite them unmercifully. Problems cause people to do more swatting than connecting. An old-fashioned fly swatter won't do. They need a bug zapper. Be the bug zapper. With the best of intentions, plug into their situation and immediately help solve problems.

We make things much more pleasurable by our presence and eliminate unwanted problems pests' cause. Be the solution that keeps them from spraying something on their uncomfortable problems to get some relief from the pests. Pesty people only seek to discover what they can take from others. The mosquito engages human skin to feed. The itchy, red bite is what they leave behind. Some have the same approach, connecting only to take and leave a mark behind after flying away. Bug zappers repel pests as well.

Amazingly, pests see what happens to other pests and decide it isn't wise to get near the bug zapper. They fly away and wreck another party rather than hang out and get zapped. Some people exist merely to wreck the parties of others. A bug zapper doesn't care about surroundings or what flies in. It exists to rid pests. Connecting to engage with others first solves pest problems for good.

Problem solvers attract people they can help. When someone gets a product that solves a problem, people they know with the same problem obtain the same solution. In some areas of our country, bug zappers are wildly popular. It offers the best pest solution. When we have a reputation of solving problems, we are wildly popular among people who value what we do. If someone has a problem they're stumped by and know someone they believe can help, they connect. We engage with bug zappers. In my phone, I have a working list of people that I call with nuisance problems. Dad taught me to find and connect with people that provide solutions.

Engaging with problem-solvers is an incredible connecting bridge. In business, customers engage with companies known to be problem solvers. In connecting, be problem solvers. Offer the right solutions for connections keep the pests away that keep them up at night. Be the bug zapper.

Being a bug zapper in the lives of others gets their attention and draws them in.

---

### CONNECTING CONCEPTS

➢ **Focus first on how a problem affects the other person**—Help them explore their feelings.
➢ **Remind positively that problems are temporary**--Build a hopeful solution.
➢ **Embrace and empathize the fear in implementing the solution**—Address and bury. Fear can't survive in the midst of hope.

---

## CAPTURE ATTENTION, CAPTIVATE PEOPLE.

Dad never had trouble getting my attention. When I was a kid, it was a distinctive whistle. As a teenager and throughout my adult life, it was, "BUCK!" I was a 40-year old parent getting called by my childhood nickname. Dad had no trouble getting attention when he wanted it. Being the youngest of 12 children, Dad fought for attention from his much older siblings with children of their own. Dad taught me at an early age being unique and captivating gets attention. As a Public Address Announcer for my son's Christian school, I'm a key conduit to the action on the court. When I speak, the gymnasium pays attention. I don't "crack the mic" unless there's something important to be relayed. During a game, a PA announcer announces the starting lineups, tells the crowd about certain rulings made by Referees and work in Sponsorship announcements. From the moment people enter the gymnasium, I seek to capture attention.

In a crowded world, gaining attention is impossible. People and companies create content to attract attention. In business, engaging means attracting customers' attention in an attempt to cause them to buy their product or service. Engaging for attention is daunting when many barriers exist. The right messaging either hits the target or misses horribly. When I do PA for a game, I transmit information to the crowd, try to create a great atmosphere and enhance excitement after a great play by the home team. In connection, we hope we're engaging enough for others to be attentive to the information we share. Information transmitted in an interaction is related to either personal or professional things. There are times we have a limited window to transmit our message out and engage the other person for that moment in time. In a typical High School basketball season, I do 12-15 Home games. Each home game, we recognize sponsors that support the school financially. I have to engage the crowd and capture attention so the sponsor's message gets heard. In many interactions, we have one shot to grab the other person's attention and keep it to avoid our message being drowned out by other voices.

There's a vast difference in gaining attention and conveying messaging that *captures and engages* attention. Consider an Elevator pitch. An Elevator pitch tells succinctly what we do and how we do it. A great Elevator pitch takes 15-30 seconds to make a compelling statement that captures attention and delivers value. The challenge is consistent delivery of that quick messaging leaving others clamoring for more. Attention spans today are shorter than ever. We may only have 15-seconds to engage and capture attention before the other person moves on mentally. Make it count.

On LinkedIn, I have a Video series called "60 Seconds with Sexton." Feel free to check it out. The videos cover a topic in 60 seconds. There's more I could say but I risk losing the audience. It's why it's not "Six Hours with Sexton." It's also why many prefer glancing at a text instead of listening to a Voicemail. At my church, a Preacher speaking on Wednesday nights, is no more than 20-25 minutes. Don't wear out people there for a Mid-week Spiritual refreshing. My goal is 15-20 minutes. If I can't engage our congregation for 15 minutes, I've failed. I must stay on message, be engaging, keep attention without wasting time on fluff and filler and get to the meat of the message.

In a crowded world, we have seconds to get to the message meat. What we only had seconds in each interaction? People process in seconds whether or not they'll invest more time engaging further. People have lives to live. Capture their attention, do it quickly, and engage powerfully. People readily engage those who don't waste their time on those who have nothing to say. People hear who they want to hear from and are eager to hear them. Engagement is vital to life. In business, customers buy from companies that engage them and mastering their attention. People do the same. Every interaction should skillfully contain those components, captivating people and have them taking notice. Engage in excellent ways with excellence. Engaging in the business of people is the greatest business in the world, making us rich beyond our wildest dreams.

## CONNECTING CONCEPTS

➢ **Build intense excitement in each interaction**—It gives others no choice but to respond.
➢ **Resonating language engages others in the moment**—It grabs attention and doesn't let go.
➢ **Remember and repeat what captivates others in interactions**—Repetition fosters consistency and creates comfort.

The four people that always captured Dad's attention: His grandchildren.
(Pictured: Standing-Bryce Sexton, Seated-Braley and Allie Poff and Carli Reynolds.)

# CHAPTER 7

## *People Buy Authenticity*

One Summer night in 1985, Dad, myself and another family went to Cincinnati, Ohio to see the Cincinnati Reds and the Los Angeles Dodgers. In those days, fans got to the ballpark early to see the opposing team take Batting practice and to see the Reds warm up. The stands started filling and we made our way to our seats as the Dodgers on the field. Fans, especially Out-of-towners, liked arriving for Batting practice for a chance to get autographs from players or a ball hit into the stands. Fortunate fans got a ball signed by a player, which was a Lottery-winning moment. Sitting in the seats in Center field, we watched a Dodger hit a ball that rolled to the outfield wall. We looked down and saw a Dodger, Reggie Williams, pick it up. Dad yelled to him, "Reggie, you're my favorite player. Throw me up a ball." This wasn't true at all.

Dad barely knew who Reggie Williams was. Frankly, most diehard Dodger fans didn't know Reggie Williams. It was enough to prompt Reggie to turn and toss the ball up to Dad, causing us to lose our minds cheering and screaming. Dad responded, "Thank you, Reggie!" Reggie tipped his cap. Night made. We all wanted to hold the ball. I kept it in my room until I wanted to throw with it. If a kid got a ball from a Major League Baseball game, they NEVER played catch with it. It was an authentic ball. It was like Mom's pretties. It stayed in the house. I got brave and took the ball outside to play catch with Dad. Dad looked at it and said, "Isn't this the ball we got in Cincinnati?" Busted. Fortunately, I had a couple other balls from later trips and it became okay to play catch with that ball. Dad's initial trepidation was the ball's authenticity. We couldn't go to a Sporting goods store and get another one. The only way a ball like that was procured was at a game. Authentics aren't supposed to be found on every corner.

Are we authentic to others? Are we completely who we say are and represent? Authenticity is becoming rare. Swiss Psychiatrist and psychotherapist Carl Gustav Jung said, "The privilege of a lifetime is to become who you truly are." For some, authenticity is developed over time when finally discovering the person God created them. There are things about me consistent throughout my life, but many things about me have been developed over the years making me the authentic person I am today. I'd rather be consistent than wealthy. Consistency and authenticity go hand in hand. We desire to surround ourselves with genuine people. Far too many times we've been duped by those who aren't who they claim to be.

People enjoy interacting with those who have authentic thoughts not regurgitated from others. Authentic people say what they believe, act out and verbalize where those beliefs originate, who influenced those beliefs and why. Some call it "Shooting Straight." Most Straight Shooters I know respect their audience and their differing beliefs. At the end of the day, they care about people more than opinions. To Jung's point, authentic people are shaped by every interaction, experience, victory and defeat they've experienced in life. In connection, we crave authenticity as much or more than consistency.

Let's advance through this chapter on authenticity.

## Knock off "Knock Offs."

In 2013, the National Football League, United States Immigration and Customs Enforcement, United States Customs and Border Patrol and the United States Postal Service partnered in a sting operation called "Operation Red Zone." The operation seized "knock-off" NFL jerseys before entering the US marketplace to awaiting customers. During this investigation, independent Online retailers bought "Authentic" jerseys for $20-30 from Chinese wholesalers and sold them online for $50-60, undercutting Authorized outlets who sold similar jerseys for $150-200. The NFL, Nike, its Authorized supplier, and Major Retail partners argued they were injured economically by those committing fraud not selling the Officially Licensed product advertised online. According to a January 31, 2013 ESPN.com story, Fanatics, who runs the merchandising part of the NFL.com website, was projected to do $1 Billion dollars in jersey and apparel sales for the year. The "knock-off" dealers cut into that number by the tens of millions with fake product. The story detailed over 4,200 websites that sold "knock-off" NFL jerseys shut down by the operation. The NFL and Nike wanted fans to buy the "official" product from the "official" channels at "official" prices.

We've all purchased items supposed to be an original or authentic, only to find it a fake or "knock off. Those sellers typically sell items at a fraction of the price by attracting buyers thinking they're getting a deal. Some sellers try getting full retail value for the fake or generic item. Generic brands, sold in the Grocery industry, are made with similar or slightly less quality than a Name-brand at a lower price. Often, the Name-brand packer actually produces the generic in a different formulation or recipe. At discount grocers, the items may be irregular pieces or cuts or smaller sizes than the Name-brand. Quality or flavor is exchanged for the lower price. Shop at Walmart or Target for running or basketball shoes. There's no Nike, New Balance or Adidas. Instead, the customer can get a discounted store brand. These shoes aren't designed for performance and durability, rather, for price. Knock-offs are never purposed for a long-term solution. Run in the Walmart shoes, and they'll do for a little while, but the joints will pay for it if used long-term. They just don't hold up. I've found myself on the wrong end of too many knock offs. Now, I choose authentic brands for the value, quality and consistency I get from them. I know what I'm getting and know it will last. People value authentic, consistent, lasting interactions and will go out of their way to get them.

There's an inherent trust placed in us that we are who and what we say and represent. In connection, we have a responsibility to others to be authentic. How can we expect not only connection but also trust if we aren't authentic? Knock-offs hurt everyone in the relationship. In the short-term, there's gain to be made being a knock-off. One of America's greatest Presidents, Abraham Lincoln said it best. "You can fool all the people some of the time, but you cannot fool all the people all of the time." Temporarily, we gain false trust making false claims simply to connect. If something looks and feels too good to be true, it likely is.

Some connectors are knock-offs because they possess no other way of gaining and building lasting trust. It's hard to be authentic, so they take the easy way out. Online merchants who sold knock-off jerseys didn't have to do all the other things the Official retailers did in reaching customers. They simply posted pictures on a website of jerseys that looked real or bought Ad space on other sites and deeply undercut the price. Everybody wins, right? Wrong. Relationships suffer when knock-offs run wild.

Here's an authentic statement to chew on: Knock-offs aren't willing to put the work in to *earn* trust. 18th Century English writer, Charles Caleb Colton, said, "Imitation is the sincerest form of flattery." That's true unless one is trying to dupe the masses. At that point, the masses despise knock-offs. No one wins in the knock-off game of relationship building. Quality suffers when people are knock-offs. Word gets out. They develop a reputation of poor quality, inconsistency and a trail of angry, unsatisfied, cheated connections. Is it really worth it? If someone's a knock-off now, typically, they'll always be one.

People trust authentic people and know what to expect from them. Be a connection people rave about. Make the same experience with each interaction be like the day a fan gets that Authentic jersey of their favorite player. It's like Christmas. They can't wait to put it on and show everyone. They don't flaunt knock-offs. They show everybody the real thing! Be authentic! Knock-off connectors go to great lengths to avoid deep conversations.

---

### CONNECTING CONCEPTS

- ➤ **Make every interaction as though initially meeting that person**--The joy should be genuine and palpable.
- ➤ **Don't imitate others**--Stay authentic at all times.
- ➤ **Promote quality interactions for the other person**—Be authentic every time.

---

## GO DEEP IN CONVERSATIONS.

I learned deep conversation from Dad. Growing up, Dad and I had incredible conversations riding in the car talking about anything. Dad asked my thoughts about the Cincinnati Reds, Cincinnati Bengals, Marshall Thundering Herd, church or anything else on his mind. Even into adulthood, we picked up those conversations. During our 10 months working together, we spent hours each day traveling and talking. In hindsight, I should've recorded those conversations just to hear Dad's voice. I have similar conversations with my son when we're together. There's something about Father and Son Time and deep conversations. Today, I can have an informed, well-thought out and well-articulated conversation with anyone at any time. The conversations with Dad prepared me and I practice conversations when in the car by myself. I practice pitch, delivery and pacing, three things vitally important to deep conversations.

A deep conversation with Mom unearthed information I hadn't known previously. It was just she and I talking at her house after coming back from dinner. I was in a neighboring town for business and visited a bit longer before returning back to the hotel. We talked about Dad and hereditary health issues. The Sextons have a history of heart issues going back to my Grandfather's sudden death in 1957 and a Sexton cousin's sudden death in 2007. After Dad died, my doctor began ordering testing every three to five years to make sure my heart is in good, working order. After Dad's pacemaker was installed in May 2012 to fix those hereditary issues, Mom traveled with him each week. She went to wake Dad to start that fateful day of his passing, but he didn't get up.

The coroner ruled Dad's death of Natural causes. I believed and told people Dad's heart simply stopped. Since he only had a pacemaker keeping his heart in rhythm, there was nothing to catch the stopped heart and jump-start it. Mom explained to me in that conversation she believed Dad died of a pulmonary embolism. She wasn't a Medical expert by any stretch of the imagination but told me Dad stopped taking his Blood-thinning medication shortly after his pacemaker was installed. He didn't like how it made him feel. Having that deep conversation with Mom unearthed something I didn't know. I didn't have all the facts surrounding my Dad's untimely death but Mom did. Deep conversations go places that unearth mysteries. Never be afraid to have them. Seek to have them often with those we cherish most.

Deep conversations happen with people on any number of subjects. Those conversations, at times, lead to a problem we're trying to solve or subject we hadn't planned on tackling. A temptation we must avoid, though, is feeling we have to dazzle others with our verbal footwork, showing them how intelligent and brilliant we are. Repress the feeling of pride in the moment and be keenly aware that what we're saying is striking just the right chord in others. Trying to impress leads to more shallow conversations than deep connecting conversations. Deep connecting conversations are powerful and intoxicating. When we expound on things and make real impact, it's a powerful feeling. I've never been a great athlete, but in moments like that, I feel like one.

Conversations like that with others take us to places we've never been and things we've never experienced. It's an incredible feeling to connect with another human being from a different background than us like a great athlete feels in a moment of triumph. It's exhilarating. Conversations do that in a way nothing else does. I can talk to a long-time friend and reminisce about someone we knew or someone we worked with, and immediately go back to that time and place. I see the sights, feel the atmosphere and sense my thoughts and feelings at that time. Conversations take us to wonderful times and places or remind us of obstacles we've overcome and emotions we faced through them.

I enjoy Talk radio. Great Talk hosts have the ability to carry a conversation on a topic, provoke thought and elicit reaction. Rush Limbaugh, Tom Roten, Colin Cowherd and Clay Travis are my favorites. Each does three hours of Live radio every day covering a myriad of topics, although listeners tune in to hear their perspective on *certain* topics. Limbaugh can talk intelligently about sports since he's an avid sports fan and worked in Pro sports early in his career. His audience listens for his opinion on the President's handling of Foreign policy. Cowherd can talk Societal issues, but his audience wants his take on the NFL or the NBA. Travis' brilliance is bridging the gap between Sports, Culture and Politics. Roten talks deftly about National and Local stories and is a great interviewer.

Talk hosts not only provide their unique perspectives, but also conversations they provoke with their audiences. They aren't telling people how to think but make people think. They make the audiences want more interaction through deep conversations. They challenge people to think deeper about subjects, not regurgitate other opinions in the marketplace of ideas. Audiences want unique voices that engage in deep conversations. I'm not interested in opinions of WHAT happened on the field, court or Political policies, I'm interested in the WHY. I'm interested in hearing something I hadn't considered and why I hadn't considered it. These hosts engage audiences, not give audiences things they already know.

The greatest conversations we have with people are those that leave them satisfied and wanting more engagement and enrichment.

These interactions add to us and others. They're learning opportunities to leave interactions far smarter and do the same for others. These conversations provide windows to the souls of others. When searching for a spouse there should be more than just a "what do you want from a mate" conversation. What life could be after marriage is a deep conversation. My wife typically isn't into deep conversations. When people say "Opposites attract," that's true for us. My wife didn't say much to me on our first date. She said a little more on our second date. She said more after that. When she's interested, she's developed the ability over time to have really deep conversations with me. She knows when I like thought-provoking conversations and knows the times I don't want to talk.

Some people don't do well with deep conversations. That's okay. Find out what moves them to deep conversation. Never use coercive tactics to evoke deep conversations. People move themselves into deep conversation by getting them talking first and talking about what they want to discuss. At that point, we become a human voice recorder. Listen, file away the information and use it to bring about the deepest conversations. Real people love real, deep conversations. Real connectors live for deep conversations.

## CONNECTING CONCEPTS

➢ **Focus on foundations that deeply connect us to others**--All relationships start with a foundation.

➢ **Deep conversations aren't forced**--Let them happen. Start small and build to deep.

➢ **Don't talk to dig deeper**--Deep conversations come when they flow normally.

## FIND REAL VALUE IN REAL PEOPLE.

As a kid, I watched a television show "Real People." Real People, launched in 1979, was the first Reality show. It featured ordinary people who did extraordinary things, had unique occupations or hobbies or had extraordinary stories. Each episode, hosts traveled to interviewed those featured about what made them so unique. Ironically, Real People launched the career of Fitness guru, Richard Simmons. In 1980, to compete with Real People, "That's Incredible" aired on ABC and took a different direction with Live performances of those with unusual talents, performing stunts, and in some cases, reenacting paranormal events. Incredible introduced five-year old golfing prodigy, Eldrick "Tiger" Woods who demonstrating his amazing putting skills, John Moschitta, Jr, who, at the time, was the "World's Fastest Talker" and "Mr. Escape" Steve Baker. More unbelievably talented people were featured that no one ever knew or heard about until either show aired. Both shows not only told great stories, but also had millions of viewers tune in each week to find out who they'd see next. Their beauty was featuring authenticity.

Those profiled each week weren't household names nor handsomely paid to perform like athletes, entertainers or actors and actresses; they just did incredible things. The "15 minutes of fame" they received didn't change who they were before a television show approached them. There were no memes to celebrate or ridicule them, nor cell phones to capture those moments. The majority of those featured faded back into obscurity. Their appearance on those shows, though, were great front-porch or dinner-table stories shared with others years afterwards. America may have forgotten them. Those Real people never forgot the authentic experience of a lifetime being on National television. American society has always been drawn to authenticity, even in an "influencer" culture. We've grown tired of packaged celebrities, auto-tuned singers and scripted athletes talking in soundbites or clichés. Our connections are no different.

People crave authentic interaction. In business, customers desire transactions with real people that leave them feeling appreciated and important. People don't want to connect transactionally, but authentically. People desire honest interactions allowing them freedom in relationships without hidden agendas. In other words, keep it real. We have an obligation to be real with others. Being real isn't politically correct or follows a textbook script. What is does, though, is builds solid, well-constructed connective bridges allowing crossing to complete alignment. By making every interaction real, people get complete experiences enhancing fulfillment in them. It's like Comfort food. Who doesn't love comfort food? It makes us feel good, full, satisfied and warms our bellies and hearts. Those dishes connect with genuine experiences and emotions from times past. Real people desire to connect with real people and real things. Authentic interactions allow the same comfort-filled emotions to resonate within others. If comfort-filled interactions don't move us to authenticity, being labeled as a fake, phony or ingenuine will. No one wants to carry that label, professionally or personally. Being real builds confidence not only about us but in us. When people know we are who we say and what we say, they're drawn to us.

In a world constantly attempting attention, authenticity gets us noticed. Not to be political, but let's look at the 2016 Presidential election. Donald Trump, the Celebrity businessman, entered the race in late 2015 as a Republican. Trump, through Social media, tested the waters first. On Twitter, followers tweeted Trump asking him to consider a Presidential run. He simply responded with a "Thank you." He brilliantly and authentically connected with potential voters. I don't admire everything Trump has done in his life and career, but his success is unquestioned. Authentic people are gracious responders. Trump's authenticity connected with voters, even in Democratic strongholds. Those voters saw Hillary Clinton's accomplishments as First Lady, United States Senator from New York and Secretary of State but didn't believe in her authenticity. It cost her the highest office in the land. It doesn't matter if running for President of the United States, selling food, ministering or building relationships, people want authenticity. It isn't hard to be authentic, it just takes intention. Desire to fool some of the people some of the time, as Abraham Lincoln said, and we will. We'll fool them for a short time until another axiom kicks in. "Fool me once, shame on me. Fool me twice, shame on you." Fools fade quickly. Authenticity is rooted in quality that lasts and is fool-proof. Anyone can be authentic.

In relationships, fakes get flushed out. The term "Fake news" has taken root in our society. Sensational stories too good to be true often are. "Journalists" rush so quickly to break a story, they fail to report the truth. Fake people get exposed quickly. To succeed in life, business, sales or any other profession, be real, genuine and authentic. Run to authenticity wherever and whenever it exists. Demand and deliver authenticity in return. When we're authentic, it comes back to us. People mirror behaviors that return results. Purpose each day to be authentic. Authenticity requires complete transparency and honesty with ourselves and others.

Real people don't hide behind avatars or photoshop themselves to be something they're not. They're unashamedly authentic and don't apologize for it. Start an authentic revolution by delivering authentic interactions with real people. Good, old-fashioned authenticity fixes a multitude of people problems. In every interaction, authentic autographs are always the most valuable.

---

## CONNECTING CONCEPTS

- ➢ **Represent real**--Some people try to find something fake in others. Make that impossible.
- ➢ **Say things clearly**--Avoid vague language and topics that raises doubt about our authenticity.
- ➢ **Don't tell all**--Share deeply personal things if it connects. Some things are no one's business.

---

## AUTOGRAPH EVERY INTERACTION.

I remember my first Major League baseball game in 1977 attending with my family in Cincinnati, Ohio to see the Cincinnati Reds play the San Francisco Giants. I was five and my sister, Kelley, was two. A few years later, our parents took us back for a Reds game on Memorial Day. The Reds were taking on the Giants again. We got there early and I wanted to get autographs. Before games, many kids and fans would gather to the left and right of both the First base and Third base dugouts as the players would sign items. Back then, I was developing my fandom for individual players. The Reds still had the greatest Catcher of All-time, Johnny Bench, Dave Collins, Dan Driessen, Ray Knight, and Mario Soto, the Ace of the pitching staff. Bench was my favorite player, but I also liked Soto. Dad, as he normally did, bought a program to keep score, because that's what fans did at a ball game. We'd also buy a souvenir, which, for me, was always a plastic Batting helmet of another team.

At this game, Dad took me down to the First base dugout area where the Reds players were signing autographs. Soto was down there and signed my program. Then, Dad took me to the Third base side where Jack Clark, an outfielder for the Giants, signed the other part of the program. I was so excited, but after the game was so bummed when we realized I had left the signed program at the stadium. Oh well, maybe some other eight-year old found it and took it home but I never forgot the interaction.

I have some personally signed things in my home office I treasure. I have signed books by Author friends that are incredibly valuable to me. I value their friendships and some of them endorsed this book. Those works and the time they took to personalize them are special to me. In today's world many would rather have a selfie taken with a celebrity to post to a Social media account than to have an autograph. The autograph, while still lucrative, can't be shared like a picture. A few years back, the FBI busted a counterfeiting autograph ring that sold fake signatures of athletes onto various items used in the particular athlete's sport. The forgers got so good at replicating signatures many were indistinguishable between the genuine autograph and the fake. People who bought the forgeries not only lost money, but the item was worthless. People should never leave interactions with us feeling worthless. That's a bad autograph.

Each time we autograph an interaction with someone, it should be priceless. Mankind is uniquely made by Almighty God. Each person's DNA is uniquely theirs. The fingerprint is the body's external autograph to the world that they distinctly belong to a certain individual. Every interaction should leave a distinct print on people. Our autograph imprinting great value into others. Think about a check. A check can be made to a living person, their representative or trust for any amount as long as the funds exist to make the check good. The name, date and amount of that valid check combined won't bring those funds to life. Those are necessary features, but not nearly as important as the authorized signature found on the bottom right of the check. That signature or autograph is the key to unlocking the ability for the check to be deposited or cashed. A person's signature is so legally important, that without it, a Driver's License, Bank loan, Credit card or a job can't be obtained. The autograph is legal proof that we understand any liabilities and responsibilities, will follow Company policies and procedures and comply with all posted signs, laws and rules of the road. We don't sign things haphazardly and acknowledge importance with a signature.

To give others real importance, autograph every interaction with them. Personally, sign every conversation with something that compels others for more. Many celebrities and athletes practice signing autographs. This gives consistency and distinctiveness to the signature, something they can do quickly and easily in a crowd showing instant recognition of its authenticity. Connectors should practice those things in interactions. Our interactive autograph ensures every conversation has internal resonance with others and is consistent. By doing this quickly and easily, it allows the person or people we interact with to feel instantly valued, creating enthusiasm and instant connection. Autographing every interaction instills a memorable feeling in others. Make a conscious effort to autograph conversations that signals distinctive authenticity. There's no denying a Michael Jordan, Lady Gaga or Tom Hanks signature. Professional authenticators know correct signatures by comparing them to authenticated signatures, looking for consistent, distinguishing marks made each time they sign. They spot fakes by small inaccuracies or imperfections in the signature that shouldn't be there.

Our autograph should be instantly recognizable by every word, sentence, gesture and posture distinctively ours. Make every interaction so genuine there's absolutely no doubt we've autographed it. We can autograph interactions so that others look forward to the next opportunity to see us in action.

---

### CONNECTING CONCEPTS

➢ **Seek to sign**--Autograph for everyone in your network the same way.
➢ **Make each interaction memorable for others**-- Give them something to remember for a lifetime.
➢ **Thank the person for the opportunity to autograph**--They chose to interact. Show appreciation.

---

## JOLT CONNECTIONS LIKE "JOLTIN' JOE."

May 4, 1936 was an important day in sports. In Yankee Stadium in New York, New York, the New York Yankees played the St. Louis Browns (now Baltimore Orioles). The Yankee roster contained Hall of Famers and Household names to Baseball fans such as Lou Gehrig, Bill Dickey, Lefty Gomez, Red Ruffing, Tony Lazzeri, Coach Earle Combs and Manager Joe McCarthy. The Bronx Bombers, feared in the 1920's and 30's, were on their way to another American League pennant when they added another name to the annals, a

21-year old San Francisco-born son of an Italian immigrant, Joe DiMaggio, a highly-regarded player in the Pacific Coast League. DiMaggio, nicknamed "Joltin' Joe," ultimately had an incredible career, playing 16 seasons, including the 1941 campaign, where he hit safely in a still-standing record 56 games in a row, won nine World Series titles and in 1955, was elected to the Baseball Hall of Fame. In his personal life, he had a popular song written about him, married legendary model, Marilyn Monroe, and was a pitchman for Mr. Coffee, a coffeemaker popular in the 1960's and 70's.

During his playing career, DiMaggio garnered the reputation throughout baseball as the hardest-playing man in the game. DiMaggio ran hard after every ball hit into the outfield, ran out every ground ball and hustled onto and off of the field after each inning. Beat writers who covered games daily were astonished and asked DiMaggio why he ran so hard all the time. "I play my best every day. You never know when someone may be seeing you play for the first time. There is always some kid who may be seeing me for the first time, and I don't want to disappoint him. I owe him my best." DiMaggio never wanted to disappoint fans who paid good hard-earned money to see him play. It's a stark contrast from today's baseball player making millions of dollars yearly on a Guaranteed contract and won't play at times from sleeping wrong or taking a day off to rest his body. Players of DiMaggio's era played more often and didn't have the luxury of private air travel as do players of today. They showed up every day.

What if we treated every interaction as if we're meeting the other person for the first time? We'd be interested in every word uttered as if they were the President of the United States, a celebrity, our favorite singer or star player on our favorite team. We'd give them our undivided attention. Like DiMaggio, we should give every interaction our very best, creating the desire to make others feel they're experiencing something life changing. We can change something powerful inside one's mind—perception. DiMaggio never wanted anyone seeing him on the field disappointed with his effort. Why? In those days, the only way to see someone's favorite player was in person. Television was in its infancy and not readily accessible in most parts of the country. Fans read about games in their local papers. Traveling to see those games was extremely difficult due to limited access to transportation unless one lived in or near a Major League city. If a fan went to the trouble and expense of seeing "Joltin' Joe" play, he wanted their perception to be sterling and create a memory of him told fondly for years and years to come. Create "Joltin' Joe" memories in every interaction by being intensely present in the moment. It's far more than nodding our heads politely and acknowledging the words of others. It's making them feel like the star.

For all we know, that interaction may be our last. Had I known the phone conversation with Dad the day before his passing would've been my last, I would've told him how much I loved him, thanked him profusely, asked him what to do with his church and his affairs and how to carry on his legacy. I know this much. Every interaction Dad and I had the last 10 months of his life were powerful and incredibly special. Dad had no inkling he was going to die. How could he? In fact, Dad was prepared to teach a Bible Study the day he died. I believe Dad intentionally made sure to leave a lasting impact on everyone around him. He wanted to be his best self. We are made to be personable people. God gifts each of us with the ability to make lasting impacts on people whether we have a few interactions with them or interact daily. It is hard to be our best every day. No doubt, DiMaggio had days he wasn't 100% and days, that physically, he shouldn't have played. It wasn't who DiMaggio was. He expected perfection from himself to uphold the larger-than-life mystique fans who saw his exploits by what they read, heard or saw on Movie reels of the day. DiMaggio said this, "You ought to run the hardest when you feel the worst. Never let the other guy know you're down."

We need to leave our "fans" amazed every time. It isn't their fault we aren't at our best some days. We go to work not feeling well physically or feeling bombarded with problems. Like DiMaggio, we can't let others know it. They need to see "Joltin' Joe," leaving the same powerful impact like DiMaggio did for the fans of his day. We can touch others and leave them as though they were in the presence of a great connector by giving them our best. Give them eye contact coupled with genuine warmth. Give them undivided attention and let nothing waver from it. Give them an interaction for the ages. As the old song says, "Let's give 'em something to talk about." Give everyone near perfection in interactions. It's possible.

If DiMaggio did that for fans for 15 seasons, we can do that for a lifetime. We can be Hall of Famers connectors. Legends never die and neither do legendary connectors. We have the ability to have interactions last forever. The ability to authenticate every interaction is one of the greatest abilities God grants all of us.

---

## CONNECTING CONCEPTS

➢ **Consider the lengths the other person made for the interaction**--Show sincere appreciation.

➢ **Tip the cap**--When someone says something resounding, acknowledge it.

➢ **Be graceful and elegant as though the interaction were regal**--People admire graceful interactions that leave them in awe.

Me, Shad and Paul Holley and Dad. They were in
Cincinnati with us when we got the ball thrown to us.

# CHAPTER 8

---

# *People Buy Uniqueness*

The word unique is an over-utilized word. What do we mean by unique? It's frequently used in describing something never seen before or completely rare. God designed people uniquely to make impact. Impact is made in life and when we die, part of that unique impact dies with us. Although we may leave offspring, they won't make the same unique impact like us. They can't be. God made them uniquely, too. While 50% of me came from Dad, I'm not him. When he died, some things died with him. I have many of his characteristics physically, intrinsically and emotionally, but I'm not Jerry Sexton. I'm Brian Sexton. Dad believed in my unique talents and abilities. His job, he felt, was to harness them to greater levels. As a College student, Dad told people he had his foot firmly in my backside ensuring I finished my degree. That was his "unique" contribution. Completing my second degree, an MBA, was all me, but Dad was there the day I walked through Graduation ceremonies at Sullivan University in Louisville, Kentucky. He always felt the need to push me a bit in situations for me to continue tapping into more unique gifts God gave me.

Unique traits are often passed to future generations. When Dad went days without shaving, his beard turned red. It's likely from the English/Irish part of the Sexton side of his family. My beard is black, a little blonde and more and more gray. I don't have the red tint, but my son, Bryce, does, in his beard. Bryce inherited that unique physical characteristic passed through me, although, the trait is dormant in me. Bryce has many of my physical traits, but isn't me. When I die, things about me will die too. We're all fearfully, wonderfully and uniquely made my God who fully believes in uniqueness. If He believes in and practices uniqueness, we can be unique in everything we say and do. The definition of unique, according to Google is: "being the only one of its kind unlike anything else." In one's circle of influence, there are at least five people that are uniquely unlike anyone else. Let's turn that introspectively. What do we have unlike anyone else? If we're honest, we'd have to think a moment on that question. Yet, God made everyone uniquely. From fingerprints to footprints, in all the earth, there's no one else like us. As a father, I provided the DNA material to help create my son in unity with my wife. I didn't decide alone how tall he is, his eye color and other features that makes him unique. Genetic traits were at work. When he has children, he'll pass on unique characteristics.

Beyond physical characteristics, we have unique personality traits making us stand out. Connecting uniquely fosters uniqueness among our connections. We have many ways of uniquely reaching out and caring for people. For years, a letter, card or phone call was the unique touchpoints between us and others, both personally and professionally. Now, add those methods to texting, Video call, Voice message or Social media networks. The impact of uniquely reaching others can't be understated. Well before the instantaneous reach of a cell phone, AT&T's slogan was "Reach out and touch someone." The long-distance call was the way to have intimate conversations with those who lived elsewhere. AT&T connected the emotions of a warm conversation and the value of uniquely reaching out. Unique connection in every conversation, personal interaction or Social media engagement, is paramount.

Make each personal touch personal. It's our unique fingerprint on everyone around us. The statement, "their fingerprints are all over this" comes to mind here. When Bryce was a child and left tiny intentional fingerprints all over the windows, glass screen door and refrigerator, there was no doubt who was there. His mother, my beautiful wife, was also intentional about scolding him for expressing his uniqueness on previously clean glass. When we strive for uniqueness, we strive to we leave our fingerprints on every interaction. Uniqueness isn't going to magically appear. We must absolutely intentional about it. Leave no doubt.

Let's uncover the unique ways we connect.

## START AND END WITH YOU!

Fred Rogers, the beloved Public Broadcasting Stations star of "Mr. Rogers' Neighborhood" was a unique voice in Children's programming for decades. In each episode, Mr. Rogers came to a tiny house set dressed in business attire, common for the day. He began each show by singing the same song, "It's a Beautiful Day in the Neighborhood" while changing into a cardigan sweater and sneakers. He wanted children to settle in and spend 30 minutes with him in his unique neighborhood and the Land of Make Believe. While doing tasks, he sang songs about different things around him or things he thought.

A song Rogers wrote in 1971 was called, "It's You I Like." The last lines said: "That it's you I like, it's you yourself, it's you. It's you I like." Rogers wanted children to understand their uniqueness. He liked them just the way they were. Those his audience were of different skin colors or other physical differences, Rogers wanted normalize uniqueness that might be sensitive to children. He didn't care about race, creed or upbringing. He spoke individually to those watching and was uniquely kind to everyone. His lesson was simple: All children were unique and he valued them. That's a profound lesson no matter the age. Mr. Rogers knew children were impacted by affirming them just the way they were.

Do we treat people uniquely and accept the way God created them? In every relationship, there are people we don't like. No two people always have agreement. There may be something they do or way they act that doesn't align with our personality or unique value system. It doesn't make them wrong and us right. It makes us unique. Great connectors find common ground and focus there. Impact every interaction uniquely by standing on common ground. It takes time to find it. Rarely will two people immediately find common ground but when it's found, it's the most unique place for powerful interactions.

Finding common ground begins by laying the proper foundation. The right soil combination of listening and understanding are crucial to dig deeper to solidify the interaction's structure. The right materials add something unique to everyone and everything we touch or impact. Without it, common ground turns to marsh quickly. There are times when some leaders forget this concept because they focus on principles over people. Unique connections are never built on principles. People don't buy principles in connection; they want a powerful experience. Leaders, leave the unique impression people matter first in every interaction with internal and external customers.

Dad instilled in me the importance of unique relationships. He focused specifically people brought to the relationship he valued most. Dad pointed out to others why he valued them and what they did for him. We have a long-time family friend who is like an uncle to me. He isn't a Sexton, but might as well be. I worked for him for nearly five year and saw his unique consistency in many situations. As Dad and I talked one day, Larry's name came up. Dad said, "Larry has the unique ability to bring everyone together and get agreement. He makes everyone feel they got something they wanted." The immense respect for Larry I saw in Dad's eyes was powerful. Everyone has specific things they value about people they value.

To cement incredible relationships with others, tell them what we uniquely value. Never connect simply to satisfy a unique need we desire but allow the other person to share that trait with us and learn it ourselves. Humans develop skills over time. I didn't start out with unique people skills I have now. It was Dad and other mentors in my life that helped develop them. They saw unique connecting skills within me and helped me understand them better.

We have the unique ability to leave people better than we found them. Remember, in connection, it's you they like, just you.

We create unique impressions with every encounter with a kind word, thanks for something or give a warm handshake and greeting. Send a text to let someone know they're valuable. Call someone to let them know they matter. Those are the unique impressions YOU and I can make. It's not hard to focus others on YOU when YOU do these things. People are more likely to reciprocate the unique impression they get from you and every interaction is more impactful and meaningful. YOU will be the one they gravitate to and YOU will be the one that changes perceptions, preconceived notions, and stereotypes. YOU are a true change agent in others. By being and connecting uniquely, we are as revered as the mythical, magical unicorn.

---

### CONNECTING CONCEPTS

➤ **Do or say something today to create a unique impression in others**—It's entirely up to YOU and I.

➤ **Don't put a time limit on a unique interaction**—You and I control our time. Make it count.

➤ **Express deep appreciation to others for their unique character traits**—You and I can make everyone feel important.

---

## SEEK UNICORNS AND UNIQUE CREATURES.

One night, my best friend, Chris, and I were talking about going to a University of Kentucky Men's Basketball game. His aunt, who worked at the UK Dental School, was a Season-ticket holder. For College basketball fans, Kentucky is one of the sport's top historical programs alongside Duke, North Carolina, Indiana, UCLA and Kansas. At that time, Kentucky was in Rebuilding mode after a recruiting scandal nearly crippled the program. Shortly thereafter, the NCAA put the program on probation and the Head coach and staff were fired. The new coach, Rick Pitino, was hired to bring the Wildcats back to prominence with his exciting brand of basketball. Chris' Aunt told him any game we wanted to see; we could have her tickets. I had a game and opponent in mind, Louisiana State University.

LSU was the cream of the Southeastern Conference, the conference they shared with Kentucky. They had size with 7-footer Stanley Roberts and scorer extraordinaire, Chris Jackson (who later became Mahmoud Abdul-Rauf) and a 7'1, 300-pound unicorn named Shaquille O'Neal. Shaq was arguably the most dominant big man to come along in two decades. No one had seen anything quite like him. Shaq was even bigger than most his size but ran like a gazelle. His rim-rocking, backboard-shattering dunks were the stuff of legends. I watched him dominate the Wildcats. It was a man among boys and I saw this mythical, larger-than-life player do what I came to see him do. Kentucky won the game that day and Shaq was well worth the two-hour drive. 30 years later, I still remember that game well. It was the day I saw the Ultimate unicorn.

Who doesn't love a unicorn picture? The thought of a unicorn prancing in a place of beautiful scenery and tranquility brings delight, wonder, serenity and peace. While being a mythical beast, it's an animal of unique origin and worlds. It's a horse-like creature with a long, pointed, sharp-tipped single horn protruding from the middle of the head. Historically, the unicorn had the ability to heal diseases and by sticking its horn in poisoned waters, made them safe for consumption. By definition, it's a symbol of fantasy or rarity. The horse has always held an important place throughout history as the vehicle of choice until the automobile's invention. It's like the reason the unicorn was created with the body of a horse and a single horn used to attack unwanted enemies. Having a powerful body and the ability to fight would be the ultimate weapon in many a century.

Creating such a mythical figure in those times would be akin to creating a spaceship or flying car. The Bible refers to the unicorn due to its an aura and mystique as a powerful, strong, warrior-like beast. Isaiah 34:7 says, "And the unicorns shall come down with them, and the bullocks with their bulls; and their land shall be soaked with blood, and the dust made fat with fatness." Psalms 92:10 says, "But my horn shalt thou exalt like the horn of the unicorn: I shall be anointed with fresh oil." Deuteronomy 33:17 says, "His glory is like the firstling of his bullock, and his horns are like the horns of unicorns: with them he shall push the people together to the ends of the earth." Numbers 24:8 says, "God brought him out of Egypt; he hath as it were the strength of an unicorn: he shall eat up the nations his enemies, and shall break their bones, and pierce them through with his arrows."

Imagine being referred to as something strong, powerful, unique, majestic and mystical. We can be a connecting unicorn to others. How? By intentionally doing what others aren't. I've made being intentional my unicorn by starting *The Intentional Encourager Podcast* launched in April 2020 and connecting with new people every day. I'm intentional about everything. To do what others around us aren't takes understanding Unicorn intentionality and keeping a daily commitment to it. The results gained from executing intentional commitments will turn heads. By intentionally focusing on what draws in others, people run to connect with the unicorn. Think about it. The unicorn has so many abilities that one alone is awe-inspiring. If all the unicorn did was go around dipping its horn in water, where is its true value? It would be a one-trick pony (no pun intended.) Once the unicorn went around the world healing water, that's it. It's still amazing, but people would get bored easily and not appreciate its true value. If we focus solely on connecting with people and not sharing gifts, we become a one-trick pony. When we unleash all of our unique gifts, talents and abilities and start affecting people, we are mythical.

It's a peaceful, serene feeling to see the impact our gifts have on others. What's more powerful, though, is how the unique gifts of others impact us. Those things happen by focusing on unique. Don't worry about what others say or think. Be the unicorn. Do amazing things every day. Do so much good people will talk it for a long time. Don't run from being the unicorn. Embrace it. Just as the unicorn knows the powers it possesses; know the connecting powers we possess to affect others.

---

## CONNECTING CONCEPTS

➤ **Let others clearly see our unique gifts and their value to them--**Don't hide them.

➤ **Develop a strong belief that others have unique gifts--**Seek to tap into them.

➤ **Encourage others to share their unique gifts with the world--**Stay intentional in supporting them.

---

## DISCOVER YOUR UNIQUE SELF.

In 2009, I became a Regional Admissions Officer for the largest Private College in the state of Kentucky. For the previous 15 years, I sold food, a Tangible product and was transitioning to selling an Intangible product, a College degree. The university had a unique Student recruitment strategy for Regional Admissions Officers. AOs, as we were termed, were given Student leads by Team members that presented the university to students in High School classrooms. The students filled out a card to receive more information or request personal contact by an AO. After contacting the interested student and their family, I conduced an In-Home Admissions interview to help the student apply to the university and begin the Admissions process. The ultimate goal was to be the school they chose to attend, the goal of every college in America. During the interview, I discussed in detail the expense of college.

Many who've put a child through college or paid those expenses might still get cold sweats and heart palpitations thinking about it. College is expensive. Many students spend the first year or two as "Undecided" or "Undeclared" majors to get "core classes" out of the way while figuring out a major. Our university was very different. A student deciding to attend had to declare a major before enrolling in classes. The university's model was a three-year Bachelor's degree program, which meant a significant time and money savings to the student and family. This point was not only a selling tool, but also for the student and family to think intentionally about college and not just a time to "discover yourself." Many students attend college not having a clue what they want to study and doing it on someone else's dime. Discovering who we really are isn't free. It costs something.

Discovering ourselves is a challenge process and one many aren't ready to instigate. It's ultimately about knowing who we are, the value we bring and implementing that discovery into everything around us. My discovery is in the form of my Personal Mission Statement: *To consistently add clear and direct value personally and professionally to everyone and everything I touch or impact.* It took a while to hone in a clear statement of what I want folks to discover about me and what to expect from our relationship. Discovering ourselves can be a simple process or one that takes years to develop. Many don't discover themselves until their 40's, 50's, 60's or 70's. Many believe self-discovery is found in raising children or their profession. I'm likely speaking to people who may be in that position. Self-discovery can be difficult. There are things that need immediate correcting and things needing more time to perfect. There will even be things painful to correct. Don't worry about the time it takes getting it right. Focus on getting things right.

Discovering ourselves and our unique value to others begins by impacting everyone around us. Unique people know their unique difference. They've taken time and effort honing those unique gifts, talents and abilities. I have Perfect pitch. To explain further, Perfect pitch is a musical term, meaning I hear notes being played without looking at the instruments playing them and sing in a particular key without instrumental aid. My legally blind uncle, a musician himself, recognized that rare, unique gift in me when I was a teenager. Not all musicians have it. When I discovered my

Perfect pitch, I worked on tactics to hone my ear by listening to songs I knew were played in certain keys and matched those songs to that key. I also studied notes, chords and chord patterns to help me more quickly recall and identify those keys correctly. I had to work on unique.

All of us have natural gifts. Without working on those gifts, they aren't effective. Eventually, those gifts die from dormancy. We must work daily on them. They won't perfect on their own. I'm totally confident in my ability to hear notes. Why? I've spent years working on that gift. Anyone can perfect their unique gifts with work. God gives us gifts for a reason...to share them with others. Connecting uniquely pairs our unique gifts with the unique gifts of others. Discovering those pairings with others is music to the Master's ears.

Harmony is based in unity. Unity strives to be unique. Discovering our gifts and the gifts of others unifies us like nothing else can. Discovering ourselves directs our connecting compasses to uniques who share the same connecting tenants.

---

### CONNECTING CONCEPTS

➢ **Discover the internal belief system**--Self-discovery starts with rock-solid beliefs.
➢ **Tune the internal value system**--Values are uncompromised absolutes. Know them and live them.
➢ **Kill the internal hypocrite**--Before expecting anything of others, set and execute higher expectations of ourselves.

---

## GRAVITATE TO OTHER UNIQUES.

There's an old adage, "Birds of a feather flock together." My buddy, Al Robertson of the hit Reality television show, Duck Dynasty and *The Unashamed Podcast with Phil and Jase Robertson*, has hunted ducks most of his life. He learned the sport and tactics of it from his father, Phil Robertson, known as the Duck Commander. Phil knows how ducks migrate, where they come from and what draws them southward over Louisiana, where he's hunted them for decades. His family has also earned a fortune making duck calls that replicate the sounds of migrating ducks. The family's Rags-to-Riches story is incredible. While on a hunt with the call he invented, his friends observed that Phil seemed to command the ducks. His calls are used in duck hunts all over the world. Phil knew from observation that certain species of ducks don't fly alone.

Ducks fly together to reach the same destination with internal GPS guiding them thousands of miles on a journey intersecting them with eagerly awaiting hunters. No matter the specie of duck, they don't fly with other birds. Pigeons typically don't fly with Wood ducks. They have different flight patterns and different hardwiring, even though they're both birds. Ducks are hunted, pigeons aren't. Though most birds have feathers, some don't fly. Being classified as a bird doesn't make it like all other birds. The gazelle and ostrich are birds that run from prey. Some birds don't soar to great heights like eagles. Where I live, we're more likely to see robins, hummingbirds and cardinals than we are ducks and eagles. Habitat and natural surroundings have much to do with the types of birds seen. When we intentionally decide who we are and the unique we strive to be, we begin flying with people that encourage, mold and mentor that behavior. It's a natural phenomenon.

Although we strive to connect naturally with others, some people aren't compatible. There's a vast difference in likeability and compatibility. There are many who inspire and encourage us, but can't help us to continue honing our unique skills. Likely, they've not discovered those skills themselves. We don't turn our backs on them but connect gracefully and strive to pour into them more than they pour into us. All beverages are made with water. What's poured into them gives a unique flavor. Seek other Uniques that offer flavor we desire. Seek Uniques exhibiting similar unique traits that we either want to develop or have already developed.

If we're in the development stage of those unique traits, other Uniques are valuable in our growth. If we've developed these traits, we offer the distinct advantage of sword sharpening. Sword sharpening is vital in helping others develop unique traits, but we don't sharpen unique skills alone. A sword is only sharpened by precise tools providing the proper sharpness to make correct cuts and stay sharp through repeated use. I value conversations with Uniques. They sharpen me. The steel that becomes a sharpened sword retains magnetic properties causing it to attract to certain metals with similar properties.

As humans, we're attracted to Earth through gravity. It keeps us walking on the ground instead of floating away. Gravitational pulls are the strongest forces on Earth. To propel a rocket into space, enough thrust is needed to break through the gravitational pull on it. The same applies to air travel. There has to be enough propulsion from the engines of an airplane to cut through gravity and get airborne to the altitude it needs to fly successfully. Gravity keeps the earth in a moving orbit around the Sun. Gravitating to other uniques is natural. It's the Law of Attraction. Put two magnets together having opposite magnetisms. Opposite magnetisms are supposed to repel, right? However, due to their unique magnetisms, they come together to stick as one strong, hard-to-pull-apart unit. Gravity works in conjunction with magnetism, not against it. Pulling together is a natural, human emotional characteristic. In the Garden of Eden, after God created man, He said, "It is not good for man to be alone." God created woman with a strong, natural attraction between the two. They were physically, intellectually and emotionally different as well. The attractive force of the two was for companionship and procreation. Uniques can form a strong procreative bond to germinate incredible ideas. Think of Steve Jobs and Steve Wozniak, two strong Uniques coming together and forming a company called Apple that revolutionized technology and communication. Their company brought a vast, immense planet together in the palm of one's hand with an iPhone. By creating an App on the iPhone called FaceTime, people could now see each other from the farthest reaches of the globe. Two Uniques created the unthinkable. Interactions with Uniques creates unthinkable connection. The Almighty, by bringing the two original uniques, Adam and Eve, created the human race. A network of Uniques creates an incredible community. We crave the company of others that function and think as we do.

When developing our unique selves, we'll leave some people we've spent a lot of time with in the past to gravitate to those functioning in the same unique talents. We attract those we want to attract. Don't be afraid of the attraction. As we grow, change and develop our unique gifts and abilities, development is evident and pulls us towards others of similar gifts. Don't fight it. Run to it. Embrace it. Gravitational pull affects. We've always lived with it and always will.

---

## CONNECTING CONCEPTS

➤ **Some uniques are weird.** It's okay to question quirky behaviors and adopt some ourselves.

➤ **Be the same person even in developing unique gifts.** Resist the temptation to arrogance due to growing.

➤ **Share freely about things learned from other uniques**. Leave something with others that inspire them to develop unique gifts inside them.

---

# LIVE UNIQUE. THAT'S YOU.

On Monday, December 10, 2012, I got to the Funeral home a little before 3 PM. Dad's visitation started at 3 and people were coming to pay their respects. This was in the middle of the afternoon on a workday. As people entered, many didn't know what to say to me. I was purposeful to greet everyone personally. Conversations about Dad made me grateful. Once people began talking to me and saw I was doing well, they began sharing about Dad. Mike shared a story about Dad leading him to the Lord and later, the impact of Dad organizing a fund-raiser as he battled Stage 4 cancer. Dad's best friend growing up, David, shared stories of their childhood. His church members talked about Dad being a wonderful pastor. Our co-workers shared stories of things he'd done for them privately. Everyone shared something unique about Dad that showed his unique life.

Dad loved people uniquely. As I stepped to the podium to deliver Dad's eulogy, I spoke about the unique father I knew and loved. I wanted them to see his unique from my point of view. I told how Dad uniquely taught me to love, work and serve. In some ways, what I thought I knew about myself wasn't reality. I believed many of the things I'd done in my marriage, family and career to that point was mostly of my own making. However, the unique things Dad poured in to me manifested themselves in that moment. Dad still taught me to be my own unique individual even after he was gone. That day, through remembering his life and in his death, I began living my unique life without him. I discovered a new self that day in a funeral home in South Point, Ohio physically embodying Dad's characteristics and emotionally conferring my feelings about my hero.

Discovering who we are and where we come from is BIG business. *Ancestry.com* and *23 and Me* are two companies specializing in helping people understand themselves better through genetic makeup and genealogy. These companies offer products and services that uncover Genetic mysteries about Family histories and nuances in them previously assumed without proper documentation or knowledge. We might find that our family came from a certain part of the world and have other racial and ethnic backgrounds in our genetic makeup or discover a particular condition passed down genetically. As we function in our unique gifts, skills, talents and abilities, it's as natural as green eyes, or blonde hair or dimples

inherited from Mom. It becomes as natural as singing, art or ath-
letics. Singing is natural to me. Some people are naturally athletic
or mechanically inclined.

Living with the unique person we are becomes normal. We'll
feel as those these things have been with us our entire lives. Don't
fight them. Invite them. Make room for them. The Bible says that
a person's gifts will make room for themselves. We must make
room in our lives for the unique person God made us to be and the
gifts that come with it. We must then be willing to make room for
sharing those with others helping them discover and harness their
own unique gifts. The most unique way to help others is honesty.
Uniques don't care about their own feelings. I'm not saying they
aren't vulnerable and can't get hurt, but they desire more to lead
others to deeper levels.

Leaders, lean in. There are more Uniques in companies,
churches, Sales teams and other groups than one realizes. There is
more talent in these places than ever. There are some who thrive
in their unique and others are scared to let their unique out.
Talented Uniques fear losing the talent or privileges that come
with it. Other Uniques fear exposing what they can really do puts
more pressure on them to perform. Lead both authentically. Let
all Uniques know their talents are embraced and respected and
there's more than enough room. Connect in that way, and an
unquenchable fire starts in them. Those living unique have much
to give to a world waiting to see it. Our unique self is waiting to
connect with people looking for unique. Life is more exciting and
fulfilling when embracing who we are and our unique value offering
to others. People buy from uniquely authentic people and will do
most anything to get to unique people.

We crave unique people that truly enhance and enrich our
lives. Chefs spend years perfecting unique recipes to offer unique
flavors. They know their unique style of cooking. They know the
exact unique ingredients they demand and won't settle for generic
substitutes. Living unique forms those same expectations within us.
We know the unique flavor we offer and won't settle for anything
less than the best for the people in our lives. Living unique is a

precious and beautiful thing. We only get one shot--no second chances. When the unique qualities we possess live through us and people are moved by them, it's powerful. We can draw a unique world to us by connecting uniquely.

When living unique is who we are, it's more than a brand or persona, it's personal, scalable and incredible. Unique people possess unique abilities and live unique lives that affect others uniquely. When the story of our lives is told, the unique life lived connects for eternity. Start living unique TODAY!

---

## CONNECTING CONCEPTS

➤ **Never feel pressured to sustain a unique lifestyle-** -Embrace it and live uniquely each day.

➤ **People who live unique lives are sometimes misunderstood-**-Reject the misunderstandings.

➤ **Fully live a unique life with unique things God sustains each day--**We are made by the most unique creator, God, who shows daily unique things He's created.

---

Dad always made sure to be there for unique moments.
May 2012 at Bryce's 5th Grade Graduation.

# CHAPTER 9

## *People Buy Motivation*

Next to Dad, my Sales hero was Zig Ziglar. I loved Zig's books, quotes and motivation. Reading Zig was like medicine to me in days I needed extra motivation to make it through a stressful Selling day. Zig's quotes were simple, yet full of wisdom. I have three favorite Zig quotes. "You can have anything in life you want if you will simply help enough people get what they want;" "People love to buy. They hate to be sold;" "Encouragement is the fuel that powers hope." Profound words from a legendary man. In 2008, Zig was part of a Live event I attended in Charleston, West Virginia, about 45 minutes away. The seminar featured other speakers in 10-15-minute sets sharing highlights of their work and offering the crowd opportunities to buy their products. Although they were great speakers with great information, I was there to see Zig.

Even in his 80's and suffering early dementia, Zig was still masterful in delivery and motivation. He captivated and motivated me from his first words. His daughter, Julie, traveled with him and was a vital part of his presentation. Julie structured Zig's presentation in a Question and Answer format asking her father questions that triggered quotes and anecdotes delivered so often,

PEOPLE BUY FROM PEOPLE

they were seared in his memory. Yet, Zig made each word feel as fresh as though he thought of it intentionally for that audience. As Zig spoke, I started writing and kept writing and made me feel like I could slay Sales giants. I heard and felt his motivation.

In my humble opinion, Zig Ziglar is the greatest motivational speaker in our nation's history. As a six-year-old boy, Zig lost his father and sister in the span of three days. Early adversity early in life could have forever shaped him and his perspective. It didn't. Zig became a charter member of American Salesmasters, spoke extensively for the National Association of Sales Education and was a significant trainer for Mary Kay Cosmetics, a pioneer in the Direct to Consumer Marketing and Sales business in the United States. In 1975, Zig wrote the first of his 30 books called *See You at The Top* which was rejected 39 times before being published. Zig believed and sold motivation. Zig taught there was always good to be found in people, they simply needed help getting there. It wasn't Zig's masterful words that endeared him to audiences; he motivated people with hope. One of the great thrills of my life is my friendship with his son, Tom, who continues Zig's legacy by motivating and people across the world.

People need motivation. The need to earn a paycheck motivates us out of bed each day and the tasks we do to prepare for work. Accountability to family, company, customers and co-workers motivates us to perform. It's one thing to get motivated. It's another to stay motivated and pass it along to others. As we're motivated, we should be motivated to reciprocate. Nothing in life should be gained and kept to ourselves. Learning anything would cease if that principle were firmly in place by the human race. Walt Disney said, "The way to get started is to quit talking and begin doing." Let's get started here talking about motivating people.

Let's maneuver through motivating connection.

## SPARK MOMENTOUS MOTIVATION.

Dad was a Master motivator in my life and the lives of others by believing them and making them believe in themselves. In the church Dad pastored, a couple named Valerie and Johnny attended. Valerie and Johnny were survivors. Valerie was a Cancer survivor and Johnny survived multiple heart issues. Valerie hadn't sung before, but Dad heard something in her voice and began having her sing solos in services. Dad strongly believed if a person couldn't do something, they shouldn't, but when he heard potential, he encouraged it. Singing gave Valerie confidence and she began confidently singing and working on her talent. Now, eight years after Dad's passing, Valerie still sings and moves people with her voice. Her voice wouldn't be heard without Dad's motivation. It was the momentum Valerie needed to overcome any fears and be confident in singing.

Dad instilled supreme confidence not only me but others. For me, he understood the specific motivation I needed. In Sales, Dad knew the motivation I needed to sell effectively. In parenting, Dad knew the greatest motivation for me was to show me how to love my son the way he loved me. In marriage, Dad knew that being motivating me to be faithful, loving and treating my wife as my partner was key to long-term success. That motivation provided the right momentum to make those things possible. Often, my greatest motivations were not to disappoint Dad. What's my motivation today? Carrying on his incredible legacy and keeping the momentum alive from the moment of his last breath to the moment of my last breath.

Momentum has moved from the Science classroom to business, sports, fitness and other things in life. When a team turns things around in sports or business, the term used is a "momentum shift." According to physicsclassroom.com, "momentum refers to the quantity of motion an object has." Momentum doesn't happen by itself, but needs a certain amount of force to provide needed propulsion. To move an object an inch or a foot, specific force must be applied. The force needed depends on the weight of the object. More weight, more force. In life, the bigger the problem, the more momentum is needed to solve it. College Football Hall of Fame Coach Lou Holtz said, "It's not the load that breaks you down, it's the way you carry it." Momentum is easy to achieve when done properly. We have to carry the right amount of momentum and motivate ourselves to provide the right momentum each day to each interaction. Visualize the motivation and have a targeted plan to encourage. It's momentum in action. Momentum is useless without action and motivates momentum. Momentum propels things but needs motivation to move it.

In forming relationships, we're motivated to connect, but at times, something gets in the way of momentum. Moving every relationship forward is the motivation that promotes momentum. Even long-term, solid relationships continue to produce momentum. That's all the motivation we need. We are motivators for others giving us inspiration to change the lives of others. The legendary British Prime Minister, Winston Churchill, said, "The pessimist sees difficulty in every opportunity. The optimist sees opportunity in every difficulty." The easiest way to start someone accomplishing the impossible is providing simple motivation. We may be the exact momentum people they need to propel them forward.

Our world needs motivation and the momentum behind it. I'm a strong believer in Intentional encouragement. Nothing fuels momentum in people more. Encouragement is targeted motivation. When we encourage, we build and lift people. The motivation to others comes when they believe we've taken time just for them. Intentionally encourage every day. Nothing does more to motivate and empower people around us than encouragement. It doesn't have to be a fiery speech or a "rally the troops" effort. Take five minutes and uplift. Providing Intentional Encouragement is essential to great leadership and great relationships. Timing is critical. Intentional encouragement might keep someone from giving up on the dream they've put off pursuing. Expertise doesn't motivate like encouragement.

If we're connecting simply to give wisdom and prove how much we know, we're pushing boulders with pencils. There's more expertise today than ever. Yet, motivation through Intentional encouragement is low. Others don't care about our knowledge. Everyone has knowledge. They long for Intentional encouragement. That motivates them. When we motivate, momentum rises within others. When we encourage, people believing they'll move mountains. They're right. We are encouragement forces that can't be stopped when we motivate others. Nothing contains a body of water when it's flooded. Flooding turns calm seas into raging oceans. Flooding people with Intentional encouragement tears down negativity and reshapes destinies. There's no greater momentum on Earth. By motivating others, we become momentum. Let that inspire.

## CONNECTING CONCEPTS

➤ **Give a relatable example**--Find personal stories of motivation that fuel momentum and encourage.
➤ **Be positive when motivation contains correction**--If something needs addressing, be positive and don't tear down.
➤ **Keep it simple and directional**--Intentionally direct motivation and encouragement towards others and away from ourselves.

## SPEAK MOTIVATION DIRECTLY.

Two of the greatest "self-help" Motivational speakers in history are the late Jim Rohn and Anthony Robbins. Both taught and helped millions improve their lives through motivation. A great quote of Rohn's is: "Never wish life were easier, wish that you were better." Rohn didn't start his career as a Motivational speaker, rather an entrepreneur, but heard a speech that changed his life and career trajectory. Robbins, ironically, was a protégé of Rohn, promoting Rohn's seminars as a 17-year-old, Robbins became the Godfather of the modern Motivational speaker. Robbins said, "In life you need either inspiration or desperation." Rohn and Robbins inspired themselves first. They were their first customers in their careers.

Both decided to motivate internally before motivating externally. They didn't need external motivation to feel better about themselves. They made others better by making themselves better.

People connect with people who get and give results. Start an internal revolution that externally motivates others. For people to be inspired enough to connect, buy-in and gravitate <u>to</u> us, they must feel inspired by what exudes <u>from</u> us. If we believe in ourselves internally, others will believe too. Millions connected with Rohn and Robbins to uncover greater things internally from the powerful external motivation of a better life. If we aren't inspired by who we are, what we believe and value we offer, why would people be inspired and motivated to connect? If folks didn't see the inspiration from Rohn and Robbins delivered, few would've been motivated to better themselves. There's a vast difference in a gifted speaker and a motivator. Gifted speakers are eloquent and command the language. Motivators say few words and inspire the soul. Gifted speakers craft each word to show off their vocabularies. Motivators craft each word to sow inspiration in others and commit to inspire and impact others internally. We move mountains when we motivate enough to change situations.

Another legendary motivational speaker was Dr. Norman Vincent Peale. Peale was a Dutch Reformed minister who wrote the book "The Power of Positive Thinking." As a child, President Donald Trump attended his church in New York City with his family. The 42nd President of the United States, Bill Clinton, said of Peale, "The name of Dr. Norman Vincent Peale will forever be associated with the wondrously American values of optimism and service. Dr. Peale was an optimist who believed that, whatever the antagonisms and complexities of modern life brought us, anyone could prevail by approaching life with a simple sense of faith. And he served us by instilling that optimism in every Christian and every other person who came in contact with his writings or his hopeful soul." Peale not only motivated and inspired others but also motivated himself. Peale said, "Believe in yourself! Have faith in your abilities! Without a humble but reasonable confidence in your own powers you cannot be successful or happy." Peale understood people had the internal ability to inspire themselves to great things and spread confidence.

When we're inspired and believe anything is possible, we're confident. We're inspirational as we become inspired and motivational as we become motivated. Internal motivation is inspiring and easily transmitted to others. People respond to inspiration that touches them. In relationship building, the motivation to continue connecting has to be inspiring to others in every interaction. We must be intentional about transmitting the correct inspiration. Correct inspiration is treating people as the most important people in the world. People are inspired when they feel important. The most important person in face-to-face conversations should be the person with whom we're communicating. We must motivate them to have more future interactions.

Some are motivated to search the world over for inspirational relationships. If we aren't inspiring in interactions, we could be right under someone's nose and they won't be motivated to connect. For the first 24 years of my life, I didn't realize the person who inspired me the most lived under the same roof--Dad. When Dad sought my opinions on conversational topics, it motivated me to be on my game and inspired me to connect. I was ready to share and engage him. As I got older, I asked thought-provoking questions of Dad but was also ready to give him inspiration as well. I knew I could add value to him. When I'm recording an *Intentional Encourager Podcast*, I ask questions that motivates thought-provoking responses that translate to inspirational conversation.

To gain true buy-in from people to form deeper connections, inspire and motivate them to continue to seek interactions only our relationship offers them. Keep them motivated and be an inspirational part of their life, business, social group, church or Leadership team. Motivate with value and inspire with hope. People not only gravitate to great motivation; they imitate it as well.

## CONNECTING CONCEPTS

➤ **Motivate simply and relatable**--Not every inspiration has to be deep.

➤ **Find different sources to motivate others**--Don't tap the same wells each time for motivation.

➤ **Make motivation relevant**--Different things inspire different people in different ways.

## IMITATE MOVING MOTIVATION.

The old adage says, "Imitation is the sincerest form of flattery." Dad was a master at changing dialect when connecting. Dad used this technique to create instant, lasting connections. If Dad were in Eastern Kentucky, Northern Ohio, Southern West Virginia, Southwestern Virginia or Central North Carolina, he'd tailor his phrasing and lingo to mirror the distinct dialect. When I saw him use this tactic, people immediately respected Dad as he adapted to their surroundings. Replicating dialects creates instant rapport. Sounding like someone without mocking them eases the interaction and creates the feeling of being "just like them." That's a powerful way to connect. Dad was motivated to make incredible interactions through imitation. For some, those interactions in October and November 2012 were his last with them. After he passed, people fondly recalled their lasts visits with him. No doubt, he spoke as they spoke—the language of connection. To imitate the dialect of others, study their tongue. We don't look in their mouth, we study what comes from it--the way they talk.

West Virginians have a certain dialect depending on the part of the state. In the North, a Pittsburgh-style sound, since those areas are two hours or less from Pittsburgh, Pennsylvania. To the East, a more Virginia/Shenandoah Valley dialect, since that area is close to Virginia and Western Maryland. In Coal country, a more

Southern/Eastern Kentucky drawl. Use words common in certain areas. For instance, "fixin" is a popular word in some areas. Here's how it's used. "I'm fixin to go on vacation next week." In Southern Virginia and North Carolina, when asking someone how they are, they say, "I'm well. Hope you are." South Carolinians say the word "want" with a "oh" sound, resembling the word "won't." Mirroring talk goes miles in building strong connections. When connecting with people, imitating their language is strong motivation.

Imitating someone can be quite flattering. Doing or saying something like someone is quite a compliment. The late American Philosopher, Eric Hoffer, said, "When people are free to do as they please, they usually imitate each other." People imitate behaviors they believe will help them get to the level of the person imitated. Irish Poet and Philosopher George Bernard Shaw said, "Imitation is not just the sincerest form of flattery - it's the sincerest form of learning." A great impressionist studies everything a person does or says to learn to perfectly imitate voice inflections, tone and dialect. Otherwise, their impressions don't work. When impressionists study people to imitate, nuances matter, making for great impersonations. When connecting with others, every nuance is important to study.

We must learn people. People want to feel at ease in conversations. Some get nervous connecting with others from different parts of the country or world due to differences in vocabulary. In some areas, expletives are used regularly in conversations. Don't mirror that behavior. I don't curse and not judging those who do. It doesn't preclude me from a great interaction with them. We shouldn't allow vulgarity. Vulgarity, offensive terms or inappropriate innuendos are character flaws. Be wary of imitating others who choose that language. Great connectors either turn the interaction in the opposite direction or simply end it. Understand where to draw that line. That's language no one should imitate.

When people connect with people who understand them, there's calmness. It's the reason clarity in conversation is important. Things get lost in translation or misunderstood between people of different dialects. In West Virginia, if someone says, "I'd like a pop," they'll get a soft drink. In the North, the same phrase might get someone punched! There, to get a soft drink, ask for a "soda." In some places, soda comes before pop and said together—soda pop. Knowing meaning and mirroring the tongue uses language as a connecting tool. Interactions become learning experiences, allowing us to be sharper connectors. Preconceived ideas of what people sound like in conversation are bad ideas. Some of the most intelligent people on the planet sound like they know absolutely nothing. Listen to their words, not how they sound.

Don't fall into the trap of correction. In connection, that person's tongue is perfect. Take what's heard and apply it to the interaction as a seasoned linguist. Often, people will speak the language of their dreams and desires. Learn that language. We all want things in life and have dreams of getting them. Motivating ourselves to imitate language that build connecting bridges leads to the girl or guy of our dreams, the job of our dreams and relationships of our dreams. We may desire to have the customers our competitors have. Speak their language. Learn their resonating dialect. We may desire to lead better. Be motivated to imitate how others speak that motivates them.

If we desire to connect with others more deeply, powerfully and have far better relationships, become proficient in their native tongue. There's no greater motivation. Using imitating language breaks barriers between us and others. All the world's money can't buy powerful relationships.

## CONNECTING CONCEPTS

> **Don't copy. Replicate.** Copying gets sloppy and easily noticed. Replication is a smooth, seamless process.
> **Don't make a new word old and worn out.** Saying something to build a habit wears a term out before becoming useful.
> **Don't come out firing.** Ease in to using terms unnatural to us. Work them into conversation.

## MONETIZE MOTIVATION, RUIN RELATIONSHIPS.

In October 2015, I came to a crossroads. I had a fantastic position with an incredible company and total freedom. My boss rarely called and I made my own travel schedule. As a Regional Sales Manager overseeing a six-state territory, I was a Lone wolf. Summer travel was great because, as they could, my family came with me. We worked during the day and had fun at night. One year, I worked a week-long convention near the beach. It was awesome, but it was an anomaly. For the other 48 weeks, the only people on the road with me were Myself and I. That fall, my son transferred to a local Christian school for High school. His immediate goal was to make the Varsity basketball team and he did. I was so proud of him and was in the room as the Head coach handed him uniforms. It was a powerful parental moment. Sitting at a School Bus show in Richmond, VA, I started pondering my future. Do I miss Bryce's games and continue as a Road Warrior or be home every night and not miss any? Even though he wasn't there to advise me, I knew what Dad would say. Come home. Even getting an unexpected pay raise from the company, I took another position with a pay cut and came home.

Some decisions are no-brainers. There are those live life in the relentless pursuit of fame, fortune and stuff and connect with others in the furtherance of that philosophy. The Bible tells us in I Timothy 6:10, "For the love of money is the root of all evil: which while some coveted after, they have erred from the faith, and pierced themselves through with." It's that pursuit Scripture warns us about avoiding. I've seen business relationships, marriages, long-time friendships destroyed over money. I've seen people leave their faith and destroy everyone they cared about to pursue a buck.

Money can deeply affect every relationship. According to a 2018 survey conducted by Ramsey Solutions, the second leading cause of divorce in the US today is Spousal fights over money. Marriages, at times, are strained by money—the lack of it and over-pursuit of it. We've placed a premium on the things we'll due to get more money. We work longer, travel for business more and compromise family time for more money, yet claim our "love" for family and desire to have the best of life is the reasoning. Overwork actually cripples relationships God desired to be eternal with our spouses and most importantly, with Him. Many claim to put work first for their family's security. Where's the security when people we love most are no longer there? The Bible asks this question. "For what does it profit a man to gain the whole world and lose his soul?" Those relationships we vowed before God to cherish shouldn't have a price. For some, they quickly monetize what people worth to them personally and professionally. I've heard Pastors comment about the amount of money leaving their church when a family decides to go elsewhere to worship, treating it like revenue leaving a business. God help us.

Money viewed in the correct way, is an incredible motivator. I don't know anyone that doesn't want to make more money in their profession. Many have left great jobs for good jobs for more money, but, money changes rational thought processes if allowed. In my Sales career, I saw some colleagues base their service or shared knowledge on how much each customer spent or could spend. Again, the Bible is an excellent source of wisdom. "For where your treasure is, there will your heart be also." When we value what we get financially from a relationship, it's a transaction rather than an interaction. To be frank, prostitutes have more honor. Relationships disintegrate quickly when one party finds out the connection was just a transaction. Character revelations are easy in transactions. Connection has always been and should always be a mutually beneficial bond between two people. Relationships purely involving money are complicated. How many lifelong friendships, successful partnerships and marriages have ended over money? Countless.

In 1992, my parents (both nearing 40 at the time) hit rock bottom financially. I was still living at home and in college at the time. I saw it firsthand. What I didn't see was my parents destroying their marriage over it. As they began recovering and Dad took a full-commission job, they got financially smarter in a hurry. Dad was 50 the first time he made $100,000 in a Calendar year. For some, that's a milestone. For others, it's nothing. When I asked Dad why he traveled so much, he said, "I need to chase the money." Living where he lived, he knew jobs like his were scarce. There's nothing wrong with feeling pressure to produce. The money Dad made allowed them to do things they'd always dreamed of doing. I wish that for everyone. Dad was intentional that money wasn't going coming before family. When my son had a Little League baseball game, Dad was there. He was always there for his kids and grandkids. When it came to family or money, Dad chose family. In business, Dad preferred people over money. Don't get me wrong, if a customer owed money, Dad would have to talk with them about it. Whatever they told him they'd do, he expected them to honor it and reminded them when they didn't. But Dad never destroyed a relationship over a buck.

Relationships aren't worth destroying to seek Fame, prestige and fortune. None of those things last. Seek relationships where nothing is expected and nothing returned. Never seek relationships where we get more than we give. Life is a gift from God. We'll do and spend anything to keep it, especially when facing its potential end. At those times, the things we've done or would do to get money, power, or notoriety doesn't matter. Life is meaningless when sacrificing the people most important to us for material things we can't take with us when we die. Those relationships are priceless. It's never boring valuing people over money. Great relationships return priceless memories easily withdrawn at any time.

---

## CONNECTING CONCEPTS

➢ **Test each professional or any business relationship with The Coffee Rule**--Do I like them enough to have a cup of coffee if business didn't connect us?

➢ **Stay invested in every relationship**—Don't rely on others to make investments for us.

➢ **Relationships have a cost**--Valued relationship cost something to keep but return everything.

---

## FLAVOR ECLECTIC, MOTIVATING CONNECTION.

My wife claims I have an eclectic group of friends. That's intentional and I value the diversity. Demetrius became a father to triplets at 47 and plays unusual musical instruments. Dale and Stephanie, were touring Professional musicians and now own a popcorn company. Dave is in Pharmaceutical Sales and a Football official. Tim is a Sportswriter who, with his wife, adopted five kids at one time. I have friends from all walks of life and varying professions. Dad taught me to connect with people from everywhere and did just about anything. His friends were varied, eclectic and possessed unique things that stood out to him. He believed in who people were, not what they did. Dad's best friend, Bob, is a retired Master Printer. He and Dad grew up in the same neighborhood, though Bob was older. He called him "Guyandotte Bob." Dad found things that drew him and focused on those in strengthening connecting bonds.

At times, connecting is geographical. Maybe the person is from the same area we're from, have family from the same area or attended the same college. Maybe we meet people in a long amusement park line on a summer vacation or an airplane ride to the same destination, striking up connecting conversation leading to friendship. Maybe the connection happens by discovering people we both know. Interesting facts lead to the greatest connections. We all know people who connect easier than others. Commonality brings familiarity. The old saying goes, "You become who you surround yourself with." We enjoy connecting people comfortable to us. We hear it often. "I feel like I've known that person my whole life." With some we meet, the connection is just right, reminding us of someone familiar. Maybe it's a warm smile or calming voice drawing us in.

Whatever the circumstance, diversity in relationships critical. Keeping our network fresh is key to keeping ourselves a connecting force. Looking for the same types of connections make us a stale connector. We allow monotony to creep in when we're reticent to expand. The same types of people in our network limits us to people that don't challenge and grow us. If we connect solely with those who speak, think and act like us, we limit ourselves to people who can lend powerfully different perspectives and have valuable, diverse wisdom. Breaking up the connecting monotony opens us up to new experiences and ideas that stretch us as people and connectors. Loosening our grip on dearly held expectations in people not only tightens our ability to understand ourselves but also allows lasting relationships.

People come in all flavors. Some bold, some savory, some salty and some sweet. Great connectors expand their people palate. For instance, we may love Italian cuisine and could eat it daily. Italian food is wonderful with a wide range of rich, bold and incredible dishes and sauces. If we looked only at pizza, there are so many toppings, combinations, cheeses and ways to make it. Every pizza and Italian restaurant do something a little more unique than competitors. If all we considered eating is Italian, we keep ourselves from tasting other cuisines that similar ingredients, but in a vastly different way. Many ingredients are common in every cuisine, but what differentiates dishes is the preparation. If we aren't prepared to have variety in relationships, we miss connecting with people that add spice to our lives. Those restaurants that resist changes in palates find themselves in decline. They only trust what they've always served. We do the same clinging to connecting monotony causing us to be stale and unappetizing to others.

Those with a developed connecting palate seek out interesting people. In the last year in our church, we've seen over a 100 people join our fellowship. Some of those people I've known in the past attending different churches and others I've met when they began attending our church. While I've connected with most of them, I haven't connected with all of them. I continue to find nuances allowing me to begin the relationship. It's hard connecting with a large group of people at once. It must be done in stages. I've continued to add diverse relationships from other sources that bring another level of joy, insight and perspective. In my career network, I look for unique people that enhance my knowledge base and make me better. I want people that give me things I don't have, make me think and bring a different perspective of accomplishment. I want people who are Givers and Receivers. I don't limit connection with those from my region, but desire people from all over the United States and world that make the planet much smaller. Connecting with people via text, phone or video call promotes community, prevents monotony and keeps our connecting circle alive at all times.

Personal connection should be a large part of daily life. We give and gain things in conversation that flavors a day. Consistently adding unique people to our lives kicks every relationship up a notch. I love connecting people to each other and am flattered when people refer people to me. Great additions to our lives don't just happen; they are intentional. When becoming intentional in connecting with those that bring flavor, monotony is stifled. Opening our minds to connection is a wonderful opportunity to meet transformational people. I met my wife on a Blind date by taking a chance and stepping out of my comfort zone. I'd never been on a Blind date. I took an unconventional route to the love of my life. We must be just as unconventional stepping out of our connecting comfort zone and saying goodbye to monotony. Seeking the variety of connection adds the most incredible relationships we've ever known. Be motivated daily to change the connective palates of others by being genuinely flavorful.

---

## CONNECTING CONCEPTS

➢ **Don't over-season.** Great spices blend with other spices. Every connection should blend no matter how unique.

➢ **Avoid the heat.** Connect with those who bring balance and don't overpower.

➢ **Infuse every relationship with distinct, unique flavor.** Spices and flavorings bring a specific uniqueness easily distinguished by the palate.

---

Dad's ultimate motivation, his family. After a service at Dad's church we all attended, March 2011. (Pictured Seated: Kelley Poff, Allie Poff, Jerry Sexton, Debbie Sexton, Braley Poff, Lauren Sexton. Standing: Brad Poff, Tonya Sexton, Bryce Sexton and Brian Sexton.)

# CHAPTER 10

# *People Buy Memorable*

Many of my greatest memories involved Dad. I was three when I first sang with Dad and vaguely remember it. I remember other times singing with Dad as I was a little older. Dad always sang. He sang in choirs, trios, quartets and solos in churches we attended and led Congregational singing. As soon as I began talking, I began singing. Dad recognized something. Maybe he heard me singing songs played around me and singing them on pitch. My ability to comprehend things came very early in life. I began reading at two-and-a-half and have always been able to create and understand things differently. Singing was that way for me. Mom still has the cassette tape (Remember those?) featuring four-year-old Brian singing his heart out and others in the background offering encouragement. Most kids I grew up with didn't sing, especially not with their Dads. Dad's foresight lit the fire that still burns today. Today, I'm actively involved in my church's music department as a pianist, Bass guitar player and founding member of 4 The Cause, a Southern Gospel male quartet. I'm eternally grateful to Dad for pushing and encouraging me to pursue music. At times, I was reticent to play an instrument or sing. Dad never forced me, but knew how to challenge me. I learned to love and embrace my musical gifts.

Dad made memories with me and taught lessons I've held to this day. Those memories are precious. Some memories aren't as good, but many are. I'll never forget the night my son, Bryce, was born. Dad left a meeting in Detroit, Michigan, raced back to Gallipolis, Ohio and arriving before Bryce did. I'll never forget pitching in Little League baseball and Dad calling pitches from the dugout. I'll never forget during my Junior year of High school coming home and seeing two sweatshirts on the table—a congratulatory gift from Dad for making the National Honor Society. I won't forget preaching for the first time at Dad's church in front of him. I won't forget the night I got married, seeing Mom and Dad sitting together and Dad singing in the ceremony. I won't forget Dad playing with Bryce when he was a boy and the three of us singing together at his church. I won't forget the last conversations I had with him the day before he died. I won't forget the last time we were in church together. For the rest of my life, I have cherished memories of Dad and in them, he's fully alive. Death will never take those from me. In my mind, Dad is young and he's a grandfather. He's a brother, uncle, coach, pastor, friend, co-worker and singer. In my last memory of Dad, he's a loving husband to Mom and proud father to me. There's nothing I'd trade for those memories.

Memorable people come into our lives. When we seek true connective relationships, we draw memorable people. I've met so many incredible people in the past year through LinkedIn, drawn to me by a post or comment. For those relationships, I seek phone and video conversations to enhance and develop the relationship. By a consistent way we connect and develop relationships, we ARE memorable. We create moments with people that imprint indelible impressions that last a lifetime. As memories are shaped by a word, deed, conversation or situation, we're responsible to create those memories for others by making every interaction memorable.

Memories made are stored in our minds and hearts like files we keep in our laptops, online or on a flash drive. Those are the most important documents, pictures, audio and video files we don't want to lose. We make memories daily we don't want to forget. Thank goodness for technology that stores those visual memories to pass along to our kids and grandkids. Like those important files, seek to make and keep memories with others. When we're known for memorable connection, we draw incredible people to us. People love to buy memories. Families spend so much on vacations each year to connect them to experiences and memories for a lifetime. Connect like every day is a vacation. Treat every new connection as though we've just come back from a place we've always wanted to go. Memorable vacations are ones we talk about for the rest of that year, ones we compare with other trips and experiences and try the next year to replicate or take to the next level. By being memorable every time we connect, people will run to the memories we create for them.

Let's meander through making connecting memorable.

## TRICK NO ONE. AMAZE EVERYONE.

As a kid in the late 1970's and early 1980's, Magicians were regulars on television, performing on talk shows, sitcoms and hosting their own specials. Magicians like Doug Henning, Harry Blackstone, Jr and David Copperfield were the most prominent TV magicians of the day. I thought magicians were neat and mesmerized me along with those in the Studio audience and millions watching as well. Magicians didn't need help turning a ball into a bird, pulling a rabbit out of a hat or making small objects disappear. Those tricks were easily done solo. When calling on a Lovely assistant to join the magician for an elaborate illusion, things ramped up. On many of the specials, the assistant was a beautiful female celebrity from another show appearing to have no idea what's in store, but eager to help.

The most popular grand illusion of the day was Sawing a Lady in Half. To begin, the magician asked the Lovely assistant to remove her shoes, follow him to a rectangular box, climb inside and lie down. The top doors closed over her with only her head and stocking feet in view. There was an impending sense the magician was about to do the impossible, yet, everyone was being fooled. The audience didn't know the clueless Lovely assistant was in on the act. While the magician "locked" the lady in place in the box, the assistant's real feet, out of sight to the audience, slipped back inside and curled under her and remote-controlled feet pushed into place. The Lovely assistant was absolutely in no danger. The magician then placed a saw or blades into the middle of the box, as the smiling assistant, amazingly, was painlessly cut. The magician separated the boxes, walked between them and took an appreciative bow while the Lovely assistant lay in two pieces. The magician walked to the fake feet, gave them a tickle, while the Lovely assistant laughed on cue. With a couple more moves for effect, the magician puts the Lovely assistant back together. The Lovely assistant breathed a sigh of relief of being returned to one piece and stepped out of the box to a round of applause. Another audience fooled. In interactions, there are those who are Master magicians.

If we desire to be a truly likeable, charming and entertaining person, it naturally shines through. People are awed by those that touch their heart. Leave the tricks to the magicians. The real magic we give to others is being genuine. We don't need elaborate productions to convince people we're genuine. Fooling people leads to skepticism in others. Word gets around. In life, don't fool people. When people connect, they hate being fooled. We can be completely genuine or be an illusionist, letting people believe we're someone we're not. Resist the need to impress people or be so impressive folks are speechless. That's the perfect recipe for failure in connecting. In life, magical people are plain-spoken, humble, yet confident people who walk their walk and talk their talk. Never leave people guessing about who we are or an illusion of who we claim to be. The old axiom comes to mind here: "Fool me once, shame on me. Fool me twice, shame on you." Genuine people seek genuine people. It's hard to be fool genuine.

Disingenuous people are trick artists only interested in fooling others and constantly trying to pull the wool over everyone's eyes. They make incredible claims to make themselves appear amazing and have to use grandeur to draw attention. They have nothing much to offer and look to gain rather than give. When a trick artist loses popularity, the tricks get bigger to grasp relevance and sustainability. They forget the simple things impact the longest. Authentic connectors give every interaction enthusiasm, skill, creativity and joy. Trick artists can't replicate or create those same feelings.

Years ago, Copperfield came to a venue my company supplied with food. In meeting with the chef, he shared some of the contractual requirements in hosting Copperfield. In the contract, the food delivery had to be made early in the morning the day before the show. Once Copperfield's team arrived, per their contract, they total control of the venue front to back. All seats were sold with only a front-facing view of the stage. Copperfield was doing big illusions and needed as much privacy and control as possible to perform them. He didn't want anyone figuring him out. When people know how the tricks are done, they see through illusions and feel cheated. When we simply strive to amaze with simple, real interactions, there's no need to be elaborate or control. The magic just happens. Our greatest desire should be to leave an astounding indelible impression. Never leave an interaction with others feeling they saw an act. We must do more than entertain; we must genuinely dazzle.

Every interaction can be magical. Simple illusions create wonderment. Wonderment creates amazement. People truly astounded never feel fooled and are left in awe of what they just witnessed. No boxes or props, just real magic right before their eyes. Their senses are captivated and their mind tries rationalizing it. I've left interactions with magical connectors that left me speechless and spellbound. That ability is lies within us all. Like the skilled artist, honing our connecting craft where every movement in the interaction is flawless and seamless takes practice and time to perfect. The magician who's desire to amaze and astound takes every opportunity to make each audience interaction better than the last. They're never satisfied with perfect execution. They believe they can be better. They seek to create wonder.

Each interaction that leaves others amazed leaves magical memories. The applause of an audience isn't what fuels the skilled connector. It's the wonderment. Memorable interactions are magical as we make them for others. They'll remember them all the way to the grave.

---

## CONNECTING CONCEPTS

➢ **The most real form of magic is close-up**--Make interactions feel like something marvelous is happening right before their eyes.
➢ **Don't set up a trick**--Real, magical interactions happen anywhere.
➢ **Avoid relying on assistants**—We create amazing interactions with our unique connecting abilities.

---

## SING IN THE WORST OF TIMES.

One particular day, I worked with a colleague, Mike, in Cameron, West Virginia. Cameron is a small town in North Central West Virginia. Most people that live in West Virginia would be hard pressed to give anyone directions to Cameron. I don't think Google Earth could find it. We went to Cameron to call on a Nursing-Home facility. In the times I was there, it was clean, well run, and the staff were kind and caring to Elderly residents who called it home in their remaining years. In 1996, cell phones were rare. The facility, though, had a Pay phone in the lobby that accepted change, used a Calling card (a Credit card for Long-distance calls) or dialed 800 numbers. That same area near the front door doubled as a visiting area for guests and had comfortable chairs. After our business was done, Mike needed to use the pay phone for a few minutes. I sat quietly, eager to catch up on a magazine I wanted to dive into. A comfortable chair, a quiet place and a good magazine would be productive wait time, or so I thought.

As I began reading, I heard a female voice singing loudly from one of the corridors. "Mama don't allow no guitar pickin' around here. Mama don't allow no guitar pickin' around here. We don't care what Mama don't allow, we're gonna pick our guitars anyhow. Mama don't allow no guitar pickin' around here." As abruptly as the singing started, it stopped. I sat in stunned silence. I was incredulous. It was funny, but I didn't want to laugh or be disrespectful. Surely, it was a resident who had dementia, and didn't realize what she was doing or saying, let alone singing. After a few quiet minutes and deep into an interesting article, the singing started again. "I'm in the mood for love; Simply because you're near me. Funny, but when you're near me; I'm in the mood for love." I heard this song before in an old movie from the 1930's.

At this point, I didn't know what to do. I tried containing a laugh and continued reading. A few more minutes went by and another familiar tune rang out. "Take me out to the ball game; Take me out to the crowd; Buy me some peanuts and Cracker Jacks; I don't care if I ever get back; For its root, root, root for the home team; If they don't win, it's a shame; For it's One, Two, Three strikes, you're out at the Old Ball Game." I buried my head in the magazine and laughed (very quietly) uncontrollably. I couldn't believe it. A moment later, this sweet lady decided her "audience" wanted an encore, so she belted out another chorus of "Mama Don't Allow No Guitar Pickin' Around Here." One the one hand, I felt incredibly sorry for this lady and the condition that placed her in Skilled Nursing care. On the other hand, it's a moment I'll never forget. Having an aunt that worked in a Nursing home for years, she related, as I shared the "Concert" story with her and both of us laughing uncontrollably. That's a moment I'll remember when I am in a Nursing home myself.

In life, moments with people forever connect us. I never met the lady I just chronicled. She could've been a great lady with a great family and accomplishments to her credit. In her decreased mental and physical capacity, she provided a memory I've held onto for 25 years. I still hear her voice as I write this. Imperfect times in life create memories for others that lift and inspire them. We're all imperfect people, flawed from birth and will continue being flawed for the remainder of our lives. Memorable connectors love connecting with imperfect people and want to create memorable connections. Those moments could be a flat tire on the side of the road and a kind stranger stopping to lend a hand; a hospital waiting room where tragedy fills the air or job loss that connects someone looking for an opportunity to provide for their family.

Flawed moments create bright memories. People look for people who have flaws just like them. Connectivity is always drawn to commonality. As I think back to that moment, now with a loved one in Nursing care, my heart connects to that lady and her family. Flawed moments show people our true selves. We've seen people at their worst and we've been at our worst. We connect with empathy because we've all been there. In those flawed moments, encourage. A warm smile goes a long way in diminishing the cold sting of embarrassment or humiliation. When others turn and walk away, gravitate to that person. When some offer critical remarks, offer a kind word. When others ignore that person, draw human attention by attempting to meet the need. I wonder at times if basic decency among people is gone. People have flawed moments. They don't need gas added to that fire. They need kindness. People embrace kindness.

Fabulous memories live for flawed moments. We all share pain, struggle, anxiety and other emotions that don't exhibit the best in people. What exhibits the best in people is connecting to those emotions and offering hope. Hope is the greatest memory creator in flawed moments. When we transmit hope, emotions change. Minds open to the possibility flawed moment won't leave permanent scars. Hearts believe for the miraculous. Spirits lift. Transmitting hope in flawed moments show others we care past the situation at hand. It's easy for someone to speak an encouraging word; it's another to show up in that moment. I'm certainly not discounting the power of an encouraging word or telling someone we'll pray for them. It's another to put feet to it and be there.

Looking someone in the eye, holding their hand and doing something to bring aid and comfort transmits more than hope. It transmits deep, caring memorable connection that shape memorable relationships for a lifetime. In flawed moments, we can create unforgettable interactions. People don't forget incredible connectors in straining situations.

---

## CONNECTING CONCEPTS

➤ **Leave advice behind.** Flawed moments aren't the time to tell others what to do or what we'd do.

➤ **Reassure even in reactionary moments.** Flawed moments cause people to react with high emotion. Be reassuring.

➤ **Don't focus on worst-case assumption.** Believe and transmit things are going to be okay.

---

## RECOGNIZE THE UNFORGETTABLE.

This story is deeply personal to my family. For the last few years, my wife's grandfather, Sherman, (98 at the time of this writing) has dealt with Dementia. Sherman is one of the greatest men I've known. Next to Dad, he's had the greatest impact on me. He was married to his wife, Winnie, for 71 years when she passed in 2013 and worked for 42 years as a Storeroom Foreman in a Manufacturing plant. After retiring in 1984, he continued a productive life, growing a garden each year, doing small projects around his house (a house he built in 1948) and cutting grass each week until age 92. His Dementia first presented right after turning 95. Our first issue surfaced during a High school baseball game our son was playing in and I was coaching. In the dugout, I noticed my wife was on the phone quite a bit, not paying attention to the game.

During a break in the game, I called her over to the dugout and asked about the phone calls. She explained she was contacted by a Travel company Sherman called several times to book a flight to Florida. He told us that he was communicating with a friend he served with in World War II. We were puzzled, because he didn't serve in that war. Since he was 95 with no travel plan, we put him on a No-Fly list at both Local airports. We didn't know what to say or do but thought that would settle things. Maybe it was a moment of confusion. We had no idea it was just the beginning. A few weeks later, Sherman called our house (we live next door) and wanted to talk with us. He told her he was heading to Florida to meet his friend and complete a transaction they discussed and was insistent on the trip. We asked him numerous questions about his travel plans. He gave us no clear answers. This meeting was on Thursday and he was leaving on Sunday morning.

We knew, at that point, we needed a plan to keep him here and knew if he left, we'd never see him again. On Saturday we visited him. When we entered the house, we saw his bags packed downstairs near the door. While I distracted him, Tonya found the keys and hid them in his house. We were hoping this would work. It did, when Sherman came to our house at 4:45 AM knocking on our door, looking for his keys. Our world changed that day. Although our state renewed his Driver's license, Sherman never drove again. We couldn't take that chance. Family pitched in taking Sherman places he needed to go dealing with the dementia from time to time in those trips.

Finally, after nearly losing Sherman in late 2018, we relocated him to a Memory Care facility near our home. It was incredibly sad for us. No one wants to leave their home. The cruelty of dementia, Alzheimer's and other diseases that affect the elderly, is the need for Around-the-Clock care, something we couldn't provide. What Sherman provides us is remembering us when we visit. It's amazing the things Dementia robs. It robs many of their dignity in things they believe true. Sherman always told the truth. Anything he said was 100% factual. Dementia changed that. I love Sherman dearly. He's been so good to me and loved me like I was his blood. I'm not trying to embarrass this incredible man, but emphasizing the cruelty of Dementia.

Things buried deep in our minds are hard to forget. Even with Dementia, Sherman still remembers things from his childhood and young adult life. We create unforgettable memories with people we'll take to the grave. By purposefully making each interaction unforgettable, we give others gifts that follow us long after breathing our last breath. Gospel Music songwriter Bill Gaither wrote a lyric that says it well. "You might forget the singer, but you won't forget the song." The connecting "song" we leave others lingers and those that hear it never forget it. It's a tune those who know us hum when they think about us and makes them smile when they hear it. The greatest songs ever sung were written by people who weren't great singers. Great singers rarely write great songs. Yet, we write great songs in the hearts and minds of people every day the world has never heard before and will never hear again.

Our legacy is our song. With every breath in us, we strive to leave a legacy that inspires emotion and stirs the soul of people in our world. Elvis, John Lennon, Whitney Houston, Michael Jackson and Prince are gone, but their music lives on. One day, we'll be gone as well. Will our song live on? Will the music of our inspiration live on forever? We write unforgettable songs in an incredible life well lived people will never forget. Memorable songs stand the test of time. I remember songs I sung as a kid. As long as I live, I'll never forget them. People never forget memorable connectors. No matter how old we get, and what happens to our minds, we don't forget people who impact us. They're forever seared into our memories. People don't forget those that impact every interaction with their consistent ways.

To be unforgettable, do unforgettable things. I can't remember every person I've ever met. None of us can. My unforgettable memories of great connectors were how I felt each time I was near them. I learned that from Dad. I saw Dad create unforgettable memories with people they didn't forget when he passed. They were quick to recall them as though memories were just created. We can do that same thing every day for others. We can be unforgettable connectors to the very end. People look to connect with unforgettable people who create unbelievable memories.

## CONNECTING CONCEPTS

> **People never forget people who make them feel like no one else**--We connect emotionally before connecting logically.

> **People never forget people who ask about their families**--Family is the most precious thing next to our health.

> **People never forget people who put others first**--Drive interactions to what's happening in their life first and foremost.

## REMEMBER THE PRECIOUS MEMORIES.

As a kid in church, I read Hymn books inside the rack on the back of the pew. Even as an adult, I read Hymn books. I wanted to see who wrote songs we sang and when they were written. These hymnals contained great songs such as "Amazing Grace," "There's Power in the Blood," "How Great Thou Art," "Send the Light," and many others. Finding songs that I recognized excited me. I learned "Amazing Grace" was written by John Newton in 1779, eight years before the United States Constitution was ratified. "There's Power in the Blood" was written by Lewis E. Jones in 1899. "How Great Thou Art" was written by a Swedish poet named Carl Boberg in 1885. "Send the Light" was written in San Francisco, California, by Charles H. Gabriel.

One song that I discovered was "Precious Memories," believed to be written by a Tennessee man, J.B.F. Wright in 1925. The song has been recorded by artists such as Bob Dylan, Waylon Jennings, Mahalia Jackson, Johnny Cash, Dolly Parton and Alan Jackson. The song is one of reflection and remembrance, one assumes, of loved ones and memories left behind. The lyrics are simple, yet powerfully, stirringly written. They paint a picture for the listener of emotions felt by the writer and transferred through the singer. The chorus reads:

> *Precious memories how they linger; How they*
> *ever flood my soul;*
> *In the stillness of the midnight; Precious, sacred*
> *scenes unfold.*

Wright penned a simple truth in these lyrics. Death isn't powerful enough to destroy memories. Death may take friends and loved ones, but can't touch memories they leave behind.

Memories last. Even those who suffer from short-term memory loss, still have vivid, clear memories of things in their distant past. Those files are forever locked away for safe keeping in our mental memory banks. They're file protected in our minds and stored away forever. Those memories are ones we don't want anyone or anything corrupting from people in our lives we hold dear. Mother, father, siblings, relatives and close friends have a depth of relationship like no other. The memories we create with them are memories we cling to hardest. Those are the files of the minds recalled most when they leave us. Those memories bring comfort in the midst of the incredible pain of grief. Those memories remind us of those we loved, bonded with and connected on the deepest of levels.

I'm reminded of the first great loss in my life of significant impact. I lost family that affected me but nothing like the loss sustained August 18, 2002. That Friday morning, I was working from home and busy in tasks when my phone rang. It was Julie, who was formerly married to my best friend, Chris. I was surprised she called. I mentioned Chris in an earlier chapter. We met in 1989 working at the same grocery store. I sang in Chris and Julie's wedding; he was my Best man and asked me to be both his daughters' Godfather when they were born. We were close. I last saw Chris on New Year's Eve 2000, when he came to my house and held my then 3-month-old son. In her call, Julie told me Chris passed away earlier that morning from a pulmonary embolism caused by a blood clot in his left leg. I wasn't aware of that. Had I been, I would've gone to see him. I've wished for the last 18 years I stayed touch with him before he passed. We had an incredible friendship. Every time I see his girls, Delaney and McKenna, I think of Chris. I've told them about times with their dad, who died when they were small.

Recalling those memories isn't hard. Talking about a man who changed my life and who was my best friend, isn't hard. Being memorable and creating lasting impressions that convert into precious memories isn't hard. It takes a willingness to make every interaction a memory. We don't love every person we connect with the way we love family and close friends, but we can love memories interactions provide and how we intimately provide it. Take every opportunity to create a precious memory for every encounter. Lunch can be more than food consumed in the Noon hour at a restaurant, rather, an opportunity for a memorable convergence that changes our lives. A simple conversation between close friends is a moment that lasts a lifetime. We become precious memory makers by impacting and leaving something memorable and lasting in people.

Memories are a gift from God to leave with people that costs nothing, yet, are the most valuable thing we give and hold. What would we give to have those we've lost with us for five minutes? They can return any time in their best health and in special places as they live vibrantly in our minds. Make every memory precious. Every opportunity to create precious memories should be a treasured experience.

---

## CONNECTING CONCEPTS

➢ **Take mental snapshots to create memories.** We can't remember everything, but we can remember something.

➢ **Remind others of their memorable traits.** Share stories of memorable moments shared with others.

➢ **Treat every interaction as though it's the last—** What's something I'll never forget about this moment if it's the last?

---

## TREASURE MEMORABLE PEOPLE.

In 2014, the History Channel premiered a series called "The Curse of Oak Island." The series featured the Lagina brothers and Oak Island, located off the coast of Nova Scotia. Legend details Oak Island contained buried treasure from the 1700's in a place called the Money Pit. The series details the work the Laginas financed and supervised attempting to find the treasure. In 2016, the Nova Scotia Business Inc. group financed $1.27 Million for the filming of the fourth season of the series. To me, that's a lot of money in pursuit of "buried treasure." The Lagina Brothers aren't the first ones to seek Oak Island's treasure. Dan Blankenship began treasure hunting in 1965 after he read about Oak Island in a Reader's Digest while living in Florida. Before dying in 2019, Blankenship was a mentor and partner with the Laginas in co-owning the island and was a key inspiration to them. As of this writing, the treasure has not been discovered.

What causes people to risk fortune, limb and life to search for treasure? Finding rarity. People go to great lengths to obtain and keep rare things. On Oak Island, the Laginas discovered an elaborate trough system that filled the Money Pit with water to protect it, not unlike measures taken today to secure valuables.

We spend a fortune to protect a fortune. Nobody is finding or taking our Treasure chest. As a kid, my parents took us to a seafood restaurant called Long John Silvers. We loved eating there. The fish was battered, deep fried and delicious. While parents ordered food, children were invited to raid the Treasure Chest. The incredible wealth this Treasure chest offered were trinkets and candy and Long John's provided for the taking. Before a youngster felt worthy to partake in the Treasure chest, a prerequisite was to place an adjustable paper Pirate hat on their head. After all, what "Pirate" dared go to the Treasure chest without the hat? The trinkets and candy garnered from the Long John's Treasure Chest are long gone but the treasured memories of dinner with family remain.

The initial reference that powered this section comes from Matthew 6:19-21 in the Holy Bible. In this passage, Jesus teaches his disciples to pray after asking him to do so. Jesus instructed of the personal nature of prayer and not making a spectacle of it to impress others as the Religious of the day did often. He told them their prayer led to an unseen, Eternal reward.

*"Lay not up for yourselves treasures upon earth, where moth and rust doth corrupt, and where thieves break through and steal; But lay up for yourselves treasures in Heaven, where neither moth nor rust corrupt, and where thieves do not break through nor steal; For where your treasure is, there will your heart be also."*

We hold people dearly in our hearts from treasures they leave us. When freely giving of ourselves, we place treasure in others. We give the greatest treasures when done from a place of love and enrichment. Think about an inheritance. For some, it's a life-changing money, jewelry, coins, houses, land, cars--things of incredible value. Some are left with treasures that hold little monetary value like Trinkets, shirts and hats worthless to others but whose sentimental value is priceless. I have a watch that belonged to Dad. He wore it to work every day, including his last day alive. I have other watches at home, including a Smartwatch. Dad's watch is a $20-30 Timex he likely bought at a Discount store. I wouldn't take a Billion dollars for it.

In life, we appreciate things and value treasures. There's a vast difference. I have several watches. If one breaks, I buy another. I can't replace the watch whose backing touched Dad's skin. When I wear it, the part that touches my skin touched his and feel Dad with me. God forbid, if my house catches fire and I have to grab things quickly to leave, I am putting on Dad's old, ragged Marshall sweatshirt and his watch. It's my treasure.

Treasure every relationship. Make sure people we care about most know how we treasure them. Treasure every interaction. Treasure eye contact. Treasure a smile. People treasure attention. Look at what children will do to get it and what adults post on Social media to garner it. Treasure the fact that every day we live, we lay something incorruptible inside others. Treasure each opportunity to give something so valuable to others, they wouldn't trade or sell it for anything. Treasure time spent pouring into people. Treasure seasons that continue to reap a plentiful harvest with relationships made years before. Sow harvests into others innately. Human beings have an innate desire to connect. We long to have companionship and fellowship with others. This isn't by accident. God created Eve for Adam for companionship. We're bonded to others in many ways, but ultimately, we're bonded. God designed every interaction as an opportunity to impact.

A treasure impacts in unspeakable ways. In every day, in many ways, intentionally lay up treasures. Build a legacy as a treasure giver, not a treasure hunter. As time passes, treasures increase in value. There's nothing greater in life spoken of me that people treasure my friendship, encouragement and interactions with them. It's the greatest legacy anyone could leave and a treasure people will travel the world to discover. Treasure each opportunity to interact deeply with others. How we're remembered is are the treasures we remember to give to others.

---

## CONNECTING CONCEPTS

➢ **Give others treasures long after we're gone.** When they think about us, a treasure should immediately spring to mind.

➢ **Don't give everyone the same thing.** The value of what we give should be personal and priceless.

➢ **Store treasures about others.** As we freely give, freely receive. Store it.

---

CARNIVAL BREEZE • BLUSH DINING ROOM
JUNE 23, 2019

**Dad would have been so proud of this picture. Tonya, Bryce and I on a Caribbean Cruise to celebrate Bryce's High School graduation. Another moment I wish Dad was there to see.**

153

# Conclusion

At times, this book was incredibly difficult to write. I found my emotions stirred in many ways and directions. I've written this book in a myriad of places, including the chair that Dad sat in at his desk. This hasn't been an easy process. I thought I'd start writing and the words would flow. That wasn't the case. This book started out as a Sales book. I was going to take the advice Dad gave me in 1995 and share with Salespeople. I would write from a different angle than other books I'd read and saw, using my 25 years of experience to explain what I knew well and hoped it would help people. In the middle of writing, my mind shifted. Dad's advice wasn't about Sales, it was about connection.

Connection is the most powerful thing we have with others. People buy from people in everything in life. If my wife wants me to do something, she trusts that I'll buy into the idea of doing it. I buy in because I love her. She sold me on being married to her and how it would be the best decision of my life. She was right! This book transformed into the power of connection and the lessons Dad shared. Connection impacts life. We "buy" good will, feelings, insight, wisdom, advice, direction and love from others, what these things give us and fear of loss without it. This book comes from a deep place inside of me. I wrote it to share the power of connection and the incredible impact we make in others. I watched Dad do that my entire life.

I pray this book help others connect in ways they've never dreamed. My life has been so unbelievably blessed by the incredible people I've known. Some of them are on the back cover as

155

endorsers. I'm so humbled and honored by their words. I must have done something right with our connection. I'm no one special. I'm not a Rocket scientist or Brain surgeon. At my core, I'm a connector and encourager. I know that well about myself. I'm married to a woman reticent at times to put herself out there to connect. My son has both sides of mine and my wife's personality. In time, I believe he'll be a greater connector than I. My hope is this book makes greater connectors of those who read it and cultivate and grow connections to unprecedented heights. Life will never be the same.

Thank you for connecting with my heart. Thank you for choosing this book and helping continue to carry on a legacy and wisdom passed on from a father to his adult son. Dad and I are grateful. May God's richest blessings be on every connection! As Dad would say, "Never forget. People buy from people."